Arthur Fiedler

MUSIC
FOR THE
MILLIONS

Arthur Fiedler

MUSIC
FOR THE
MILLIONS

THE STORY OF THE
CONDUCTOR OF THE BOSTON
POPS ORCHESTRA

by

Carol Green Wilson

THE EVANS PUBLISHING COMPANY

New York

To

ELLEN

Author's Preface
and Acknowledgments

THIS BOOK EVOLVED out of a casual conversation with Ellen Fiedler in Boston in the spring of 1960. A librarian was speaking of her futile search for a book about Arthur Fiedler. His wife replied, "There is none. We are waiting for 'Nanna Carol' to do it." Their daughters are about the same age as two of our grandchildren and this familiar appellation for me grew out of their companionship during the first summer the Fiedler family spent in San Francisco. That beginning eighteen years ago ripened into a lasting friendship.

I have spent some time as a guest in the Fiedler home in Brookline, Massachusetts, reading the scrapbooks his sister had methodically pasted, and visiting with neighbors and friends. I am particularly grateful to his two sisters, the late Frederika Fiedler and Rosa Fiedler Hochland, for their reminiscences of childhood, and to Mr. and Mrs. Philip Clark of Brookline for their travel tales. Leonard Bernstein graciously verified the story of his conducting debut under Fiedler.

In Boston Laning Humphrey of the Symphony Public Relations Department was generous in the use of his files and his memory. The Boston Public Library gave cordial access to the material in their Music Department. George Judd, former Manager of the Boston Symphony Orchestra, read the entire manusript and gave me pertinent suggestions. His son, William Judd, Arthur Judson, and Miss Nora Shea of Columbia Artists' Management in New York assisted me, as did Alan Kayes and Peter Delheim of RCA-Victor. I spent considerable time in Boston, attending both Pops and Esplanade concerts, and made a summer trip to Tanglewood to watch one of the Fiedler popular concerts. I am indebted to Mr. Robert K. Wheeler of Stockbridge, Massachusetts, for material on the history of this Berkshire Music Festival.

The late Cyrus Durgin, then Music Critic of the *Boston Globe,* helped me to grasp the place of Arthur Fiedler in the heart of Boston, both in a lengthy interview and later correspondence. Mr. Jacobus Langendoen, retired cellist of the Boston Symphony recalled incidents of his days as a member of the Fiedler Trio. Mr. Henry Cabot, President of the Board of Trustees of the Boston Symphony Orchestra, answered my letter with cordial pleasure over the fact that I was writing a biography of Arthur Fiedler.

The San Francisco part of the story came out of

personal experience, plus assistance from the late Joseph Dyer, Secretary of the San Francisco Art Commission, the late Robert Newell who was Fiedler's host at the Bohemian Grove Encampment, and John K. Hagopian of the Art Commission. For several summers I punched the clock, along with the players, at rehearsals, where I was invited by Mr. Fiedler to sit on the platform among the musicians in order to gain intimate knowledge of his method of conducting.

The story of Arthur Fiedler's introduction to San Francisco audiences through *"The Standard Hour"* was related to me by Howard Vesper, Director and Vice-President of Standard Oil Company of California, and Adrian Michaelis, Director of that program, who arranged for me to read the company files dealing with Fiedler's coming.

Harry Ellis Dickson, Assistant Conductor of the Boston Pops and Esplanade orchestras, was most helpful in the East, as were Henry Shweid, Concert master of the San Francisco Pops, Reina Shivo, Joe Sinai, and other members of that orchestra. Ruth Slenczybska, and the mother of David Abel both shared personal experiences of Arthur Fiedler's constructive concern for young artists. I am particularly grateful to our friend, Dr. George McManus, former Boston Music Critic, and member of the faculties of Connecticut Wesleyan and Harvard Universities, who devoted many hours to critical assistance on this manuscript.

What I present in the following pages is a personal tribute to a man who has contributed immeasurably to community understanding of good music, both classical and popular for well over a half century.

Carol Green Wilson
San Francisco, January 5, 1968

Contents

An Appreciation

Arthur Fiedler has devoted all his life and great talents to music. He was for years one of the chief violinists in the Boston Symphony. During that period he was able to observe many of the greatest conductors of the 20th Century. This rich experience and technical knowledge he has given to his conducting of popular music, which has immensely added to the appreciation of orchestral music all over the United States, and all over the World through his records.

His contribution to music is unique.

Leopold Stowkowski

LEOPOLD STOWKOWSKI

Arthur
Fiedler

MUSIC
FOR THE
MILLIONS

CHAPTER ONE

Born to Music

"THAT SHOULD BE A-flat in the second 'cello!"

The authoritative voice commanded attention from eight amateur 'cellists, hard at work under California redwoods. They looked up, startled, as they recognized the unexpected silver-haired visitor standing at the camp entrance.

"Arthur Fiedler!" Their leader's greeting was tinged with chagrin as he realized that the conductor of the Boston Pops Orchestra had caught his players fumbling over a sour note in their third attempt to rehearse a special arrangement of a Chopin Prelude by one of the group.

"Please take this," he said, proffering the baton to Fiedler, who accepted the stick with zest.

Immediately correct melodious sound floated up through sunlit trees as the welcome guest continued the rehearsal. The finished performance—still under his direction—at a neighboring camp that same afternoon became a highlight of that summer's world-famous Bohemian Grove Encampment.

Such spontaneous response is characteristic of this convivial musician, who has led the same symphony orchestra longer than any other American conductor. He is instantly ready to participate wherever music is being made—whether he slips onto a piano bench to play a lively accompaniment to a five-year-old's improvised tune or, unannounced, accepts the band-master's stick to lead the U.S. Navy Band playing *Stars and Stripes Forever* in Buenos Aires.

Guest-conducting has taken him from Tokyo to Tel-Aviv, from Miami to Vancouver, all over the Americas and the British Isles. Rehearsal hours in far places are often reunions. He greets members of orchestras personally and asks about their families. If his sensitive ear catches a false note, he points to a member of the horn section and says quietly, "Bob, that should sound concert D."

Familiar gestures usually take the place of words. Thumb up means a note is flat; down, if sharp. The offending player knows that if the correction is not instantaneous a biting reprimand will focus all eyes on him. Yet in spite of Fiedler's exacting demands he is more apt to evoke a laugh than resentment. "Ask Santa Claus to bring you a metronome" brings results when some members of the violin section lag behind his beat in the fast pace of Anderson's *Fiddle Faddle*—a snappy piece dedicated to the Pops conductor. Another time when an unresponsive 'cellist fails to take seriously an excerpt from *West Side Story,* he urges *"con amore*—this is beautiful music . . . don't look down your nose at it!"

Fiedler programs are as catholic in taste as his widespread circle of musical friends. "Something for everyone" is the criterion as he turns to the large red-leather-bound books which record the exact timing and year of performance of every march, symphony, or other work he has ever conducted. From this biography of his musical life he has blended pleasing combinations which have won many awards in *Musical America's* Annual National Radio Polls.

Music making is fun to this peripatetic purveyor of melody and rhythm. It is life. It is exciting. And he has the capacity and energy to share his enthusiasm with all he meets. Always alert, Arthur Fiedler tunes in to the right wave length for each person who needs musical help. One day it was a paralyzed soldier with a tune that merited orchestration. Another time it was young Leonard Bernstein, ready for his conducting debut in the Esplanade Shell. Wherever he is, from the deep well of his own knowledge and experience he continually draws draughts of friendly aid. Through depression and war his was the faith that kept other musicians from despair. Few men have done so much to popularize classical music, or to win conservatives to appreciation of the good in tunes that are favorites with the masses.

For more than half a century he has dedicated all his fervor and talent to spreading the love of music among people everywhere. On the high road or the low road, he has become Pied Piper to countless listeners. Young and old, rich and poor, learned or illiterate, have jammed halls and collected record albums—grateful to this colorful interpreter of all kinds of good music.

None of this is accidental. Musical acumen came to him along with the genes which produced his distinguished features and the mane-like hair, now turned from black to silver. He was literally born to music as the walls of his father's Boston home echoed the tones of string ensembles. Even as a four-year-old playing with blocks in a corner of that living room while members of the famous Kneisel Quartette rehearsed difficult passages, little Arthur would clap his hands over his ears and shudder if a player's intonation slipped ever so slightly.

Emanuel Fiedler, second violinist in this distinguished group, had won the gold medal of the Vienna Conservatory in 1884. He had been the natural choice of another Viennese, Wilhelm Gericke, among players selected to take to America with him when Gericke became the second conductor of the Boston Symphony Orchestra. By the time the Fiedler's only son was born—December 17, 1894—Gericke had been succeeded by the brilliant Hungarian, Arthur Nikisch, for whom this child was named.

Older sisters, Frederika and Rosa, always described the bearer of these two distinguished musical names as a "quiet little boy." Yet they could recall many instances when mischief twinkled in his dark eyes. Rosa, nearest to

Arthur in age, was his partner in devilment. The two
smothered a frog in 'Rika's sheets, and held a race to
see how many fleas each could pull off the dog's hide.
When the colored cook hid fresh doughnuts on the high-
est shelf, Arthur piled chairs ladder-wise to reach the
sweets he craved.

Their mother forbade participation in Fourth-of-
July fun. Her children, destined to be musicians, must
not risk their fingers on fire crackers. So Rosa and Arthur, as they went to bed, tied strings to their ankles and
dropped the ends out the window. Neighbor Billy
O'Brien pulled the strings when he was ready to shoot
his pinwheels, and the two climbed down the fire escape.

When Arthur was eight years old, he disappeared
for one whole night. Early in the morning he raced into
the kitchen, his big eyes popping with excitement. Pent-
up words were ready to explode, but his mother silenced
him coldly.

"Go to your room at once. Your father will see to
your punishment when he returns from the police
station."

The penalty was "house arrest" for a week; but the
real punishment was the inability to tell the dramatic
tale of a night spent with the Indians of a nearby Buffalo
Bill Show.

His "arrest" did not deter him from wandering off
to the Bijou Dream movie house against orders.

"Only boys with clean eyes go there," his mother
told him. And he scrubbed his own with abrasive sapolio,

until they were inflamed so badly that he was troubled for years.

The children were never allowed to forget that Fiedler means "fiddler" in German. All four were started early on both piano and strings. Strikingly beautiful Johanna Bernfeld Fiedler was a "good amateur musician"; more than that, she was a perceptive teacher. 'Rika and Elsa, youngest of the three sisters, stayed with the piano. Arthur was equally proficient on both piano and violin. Rosa chose the 'cello along with the piano. Discipline was rigid. Emanuel's bow cut across little fingers in rage if one note was off beat; the 'cello was frequently bathed in tears.

As the youngsters progressed they were promoted to outside lessons. Rosa and Arthur came under the tutelage of Carl Lamson, later famous as accompanist for Fritz Kreisler. His studio was next to the police station, which provided a fascinating diversion when the window was open. More than once the children were late to lessons when the paddy wagon drew up just as they arrived. His childish curiosity was prophetic of Fiedler's adult friendship with members of the Boston Police Force!

Johanna Fiedler recognized her son's exceptional talents and humored his whims. If he was ordered from the table for dunking bread in his tea-with-milk, she would slip up to his room later with a favorite delicacy. Sometimes when he had survived a rough practice under his father's surveillance, she would reward the boy with a trip to the B. F. Keith vaudeville. Here the impressionable youngster developed a flair for the dramatic that flavored all his later career. Even at the age of sixty-eight he delighted a friendly photographer when he danced The Twist with a night club singer after a San Francisco Pops concert; and nearing seventy he accepted the dare of Al Hirt to lead his jazz band of six in a Bourbon Street night club in New Orleans.

One toy, cherished in childhood, contributed to his rapport with the non-musical world. A perfect replica of a Boston fire engine of those early days was made for little Arthur by a Mexican engineering student at M.I.T., who was a violin pupil of Emanuel. This model, with its functioning water pump, inspired a life-long interest. Arthur Fiedler, fire buff, probably owes his collection of Honorary Fire Chief badges and helmets to this gift.

Arthur went to the Prince Grammar School and later to the Boston Latin School. Here he played the drums for the school band. But it was his bow, not his sticks, that brought him on stage at graduation day. Father and Mother Fiedler sat in the front row, proud of the stance of the attractive boy who tucked his violin under a round chin to tune up for his solo. Then, to Arthur's lasting chagrin, Emanuel sprang from his seat, grabbed the instrument and tuned it accurately. Tears must have burned behind those big brown eyes as Arthur drew his bow across the correctly-tuned strings; but the boy kept his composure until they reached home. Then anger blurred his pleasure when father congratulated

him on his performance. The boy whose accurate ear
could spot the needed A-flat as he listened to a chance
camp rehearsal fifty years later was proud and sensitive.
Father's distrust of his ability to tune that violin hurt
deeply.

Despite all the success of his later career, there is
anomaly in Arthur Fiedler's reaction to public admiration. He basks in the deference of a casual by-stander who
replies to his apology for holding up traffic by saying,
"I would wait an hour anywhere for *you*"; but according to one of his closest musical associates, he is "completely lacking in vanity about himself and his achieve-
ments . . . almost naive . . . he never boasts." The day
came when Emanuel Fiedler would boast about "my
golden son"; but in those early years of parental discipline, the cock-sure father kept his children striving,
never quite satisfied.

Conversation at home was always carried on in
German. Because he learned English at school he was
bi-lingual from these early years. Facility in language increased with travel and experience. The ability to speak
with people in their native tongue won friends whether
in the vegetable markets of North End Boston or meeting an interviewer on the Argentine TV. Never a Spanish student, he managed to acquire enough properly ac-
cented words under the tutelage of the Argentinian
RCA-Victor manager to convince the people of Buenos
Aires that he was *simpatico*.

By 1910, Emanuel Fiedler, having completed a

quarter of a century with the Boston Symphony Orchestra, felt that his children needed the incentive and discipline of European musical training. A desk in the first violin section of the Berlin Philharmonic was open to him the following season.

After a short visit with grandparents in Vienna, where the elder Fiedler was a conductor, the family settled in a large apartment near the Kürfurstendamm in Berlin. In the rear walled-in garden there was another smaller apartment, in which Emanuel gave violin lessons and the young Fiedlers practiced.

Arthur, now in his 'teens, was restless.

"Papa," he announced one day. "I'm through with all this practicing. I don't think I want to be a musician."

His father raised an eyebrow. Knowing full well the grind and the heartaches that go with any artistic success, he had predicted all along that Arthur, a typical American boy, probably did not have that special urge essential for a successful musical career.

The family held a conference, drawing into it Johanna's sister, who was married to the baritone, Adolph Muehlman—later a Metropolitan Opera contemporary of Caruso. Their Berlin acquaintance was wide and varied. Through the Muehlmans' introduction Arthur was soon on the payroll of a large publishing house; but a few weeks of licking stamps, running errands, cleaning ink wells, and other menial tasks sent him home, discouraged. The promised "chance for advancement in the business" looked indefinitely far off.

"I'm tired of sweeping floors," he confessed to his father. "I guess I was meant to be a musician, after all."

"Good!" Emanuel was satisfied with the result of that experiment. "Auditions for some scholarships at the Royal Academy will be held soon. If you'll really work with me, I think maybe you can get one."

In the meantime Arthur joined his sisters at the Ochs-Eichelberger Conservatory. Here, at an early recital, the boy first held a baton in public. A yellowed program lists Rosa Fiedler among the 'cellos, and Arthur conducting *The Sleigh Ride* by Mozart.

Soon Fiedler names were appearing on many programs. Rosa Fiedler "aus Boston" gave a 'cello recital at the Hotel Kaiserhof, with Herr Artur Fiedler at the piano. Two Golterman numbers—*Romanze* and *Charakterstück*—were their contributions to the program. A family trio, Elsa, Rosa, and Arthur, was playing in the Kaiser Saal at the Zoological Garden a few weeks later.

Emanuel kept in touch with those who were planning the coming auditions, holding out greater incentive for Arthur's practicing. His father's bow rapped frequently across racing knuckles, but the results were worth all the effort. Arthur was one of thirteen applicants accepted out of the fifty-four who had sought admission to the great Berlin Academy which was then sending its graduates to every worthy orchestra around the world. Willy Hess, who had been concert master of the Boston Symphony and a colleague of Emanuel under Gericke, became Arthur's violin instructor, and

the Hungarian composer, Ernst von Dohnanyi, introduced him to the pleasure of chamber music. But the
two who molded his future were the professors of conducting—Arno Klieffel and Rudolf Krasselt.

Soon the 'teen-ager began to experience the rigors
of musical tours—which in years to come would blazon
his name on billboards around the globe. His father secured a place for Arthur with the touring Blüthner
Orchestra. In one of the last summers of a peaceful
Europe, father and son traveled together to Oslo, Copen-
hagen, Stockholm, and Helsinki.

During another vacation period young Fieldler
was invited to join a string ensemble conducted by Johann Strauss III, grandson of the famous Waltz King.
Sixteen-year-old Arthur, as leader of the second violin
section, learned techniques that make Fiedler recordings
of Strauss Waltzes favorites in many an American record
library forty years later. He also became familiar with
the music-loving cities of pre-war Germany as he toured
that country under the autocratic son of Eduard Strauss.
Arthur Fiedler remembers the bearer of this distinguished name as not too brilliant a performing musician,
but as a martinet who combined the functions of conductor, manager, and paymaster.

Back in the German capital his piano playing—
espcially his comprehension and intuition as an accompanist—won the youth invitations and engagements.
His parents became concerned as the new life kept
Arthur roaming the streets of Berlin with congenial

cronies after the parties were over. If his mother could have followed these roamings she would have had real cause for her concern. With a fellow student named Waldo Mayo these two who had "slaved" at their studies for ten to twelve hours sought recreation among the beauteous damsels drifting about the gay cafes of the Kürfurstendam. One night the brazen electric advertisement on the Potsdamer Platz guaranteed a new product —"Erotikon" to stimulate sexual desires. The boys somewhat sheepishly entered a pharmacy. They divided the box of capsules they bought and started off; but the edge rubbed off their boasting about the miraculous effect of the love potion when Mayo read the fine print on the empty container stating that the pills would take effect in seven days.

Unaware of the real night escapades of her son, Johanna—who insisted that a seevnteen-year-old was still subject to home rules—put a chain lock on the apartment door promptly at eleven o'clock.

"I forbid you to stay out later," she proclaimed. When she had to unlock the door for her son the next time, she added, "if this happens again, you will have to leave home."

That was exactly what the independent young man wanted. He found a rooming house and cut himself off from all family contact, not even telling them where he lived. The Fiedlers were aghast. They had not expected so drastic an outcome.

Rosa and her father walked, disconsolate, evening

after evening, scanning the faces of passers-by as twilight
dimmed the shadowy linden trees. After a few weeks of
mounting discouragement, Emanuel stopped suddenly
under an open window.

"Listen," he whispered. The strains of the Mendelssohn Concerto filled the street with familiar sound.
"That sounds like Artur!"

"Oh, Papa, it is!" cried Rosa, edging her father toward the door.

"No, no, not yet." Her father commanded sternly,
fighting his own impulse. "We must talk with Mama
first."

When Arthur returned to his lodgings the next
night, the landlady was full of news. A distinguished-
looking couple with a big dog had been inquiring for
him. They had not left their names. Arthur sighed with
relief, "That's them, all right!"

He tucked his violin under his arm and hurried to
the family apartment, ready to admit that home meant
more to him than pride. Johanna's beautiful eyes glis-
tened, as she heard her son tell of lonely evenings with
no sisters to play trios, no piano for practicing, no one
to make his favorite küchen. Still the boy was stubborn.
He wanted to return; but on his own terms. He was
mature. He had proved that he could earn his bread. He
was given his own key!

Among the many new friends of the personable
young violinist was an American news correspondent by
the name of Hirsch, whose wife was an accomplished

violinist. The two were like second parents to Arthur, who was on a vacation trip with them in the Austrian Alps when the Archduke was murdered at Sarajevo.

Everything came to a standstill in the small resort town as Austria immediately mobilized. Cooks dropped their pots and pans, and waiters stripped off their aprons as every able-bodied male hurried to take up arms. Trains being commandeered for troop movement, Hirsch hired a horse and cart to transport his family and guest to the border. They walked across to what they hoped would be the safety of a still neutral Germany.

CHAPTER TWO

~~~

War Drums

THE TRAVELLERS REACHED Berlin just as Germany declared war on the Triple Entente. Arthur found his father distraught. Emanuel was beyond the age for conscription; but he was full of fears for his talented son. He reproved himself for not having taken out citizenship papers during his long sojourn in the United States, for now Arthur, born in Boston and thus considered a citizen under United States' law, might be pressed into service as the under-age son of Austrian parents. He spoke earnestly with Arthur. Would the lad like to return to the uncles who had stayed in America? Yet, even as he posed the question, his heart sank. The Atlantic was already danger-filled, with German submarines daily sinking British ships. The bright future he had so long envisaged for this ambitious youth might easily be unrealized whichever choice they made. This war, rising out of the political power struggle of middle Europe was far from the liking of the peace-loving

15

musician. Yet, as a man of sagacity and experience, he recognized its implications.

Young Arthur was not so deeply concerned. The wealthy aristocrats who constantly engaged him to perform at musical teas, social clubs, and salon recitals were not yet alarmed over this "temporary military action." They shrugged it off as a situation that could be quickly and effectively handled by the men they had entrusted with the protection of the Fatherland! The boy could not see why it was any concern of his. After all, he *was* an American, and his nation had no part in it. He was making good money and enjoying life with family and friends. He would stay in Berlin.

The Fiedler Trio began to play at benefits for war victims. In March, 1915, Arthur was helping to raise money for the Red Cross; the "Berliner Tageblatt" spoke of "Arthur Fiedler's viola part played with excellence," adding gratitude that "in times of terrible war we can have the joy of music in a quiet place."

The versatile young musician still performed on both piano and violin; but the viola was becoming his favorite. He was playing that instrument with a string quartette at the Hirsch home one evening when a long distance call to the U.P. correspondent electrified the gathering. The *S.S. Lusitania* had been sunk with many Americans among the drowned!

Hirsch spoke sternly to his friend. "Arthur," he said, "The United States will soon be drawn into this war. You must get out of here at once!"

The next morning Arthur was a the office of the American Ambassador as soon as it opened. "What is my status?" he inquired of Mr. Gerard.

"You have an American passport," the Ambassador reminded him. "Use it as quickly as you can. Get to some neutral country. This war cannot last long. Then you can return to your family and your studies."

Arthur reported the conversation to Hirsch. "That's right," his friend concurred. "Be off as soon as you can get transportation. Here is $200. You'll need it."

At the Royal Academy where he went to ask for temporary leave, Arthur met an American classmate— Albert Stoessel, who in later years would become the famous leader of the New York Oratorio Society and a favorite in Chautauqua circles. Stoessel readily agreed to go with him. The young men picked up their instruments, packed a small bag of belongings, said good-bye to Arthur's family, and were on their way to Holland that very night.

Amsterdam, its streets choked with cyclists and its canals with boats and barges, did not offer much hospitality to the two bewildered German-Americans. They found a cheap apartment and set out with a dual purpose. They expected to earn enough to live on by playing in restaurants and night clubs and to devote daytime hours to continued studies under some of the important men in the famous Concertgebouw Orchestra. But they soon discovered that they were not alone in their predicament. Holland was rapidly becoming crowded with Belgian refugees, among them many musicians with like intent.

Hirsch's generous gift was dwindling. Engagements were few and far between. After a month and a half of struggle Arthur was willing to listen to his friend's urging to return to America. Stoessel was engaged to a Boston girl, whose letters were insistent. Finally, they secured passage on the old S.S. *Rotterdam* and commenced a voyage that took twenty-one danger-filled days. The ship was stopped and searched in the English Channel, where their German names caused embarrassment. Some suspicious characters were taken off and interned, but the young musicians' papers were in order. After a thorough search and questioning, the frightened violinists were allowed to continue their journey.

At last they docked in Boston. Stoessel went off to join his fiancee, and Arthur hunted up his Fiedler uncles. Gustav was in Boston, but Bernard, a veteran member of the Boston Symphony Orchestra, was vacationing on Nantucket Island. He wrote insistently to his nephew to join him in the quaint city of early American whalers, now a favorite resort for city-weary easterners. Arthur accepted. His job with the dinner orchestra in the big gray-blue and white clapboard hotel was not exactly what an honor sudent of the Royal Berlin Academy might have expected, but it was a way to earn room and board.

It did not take the summer visitors long to be

charmed by the slender violinist with his witty smile and dreamy deep brown eyes. Arthur made friends among them, and they soon discovered his prowess with a lanyard and a top sail. Swimming and sailing were pleasant diversions, but there was not much professional stimulus in those few Nantucket weeks.

When word filtered through from one of these passing acquaintances that there was a modestly-paying opening with the orchestra of the Kimball Hotel in Springfield, Massachusetts, he was quick to apply for the job. That engagement brought strange new experiences to Arthur, whose earlier living had always been in large cities—Boston, Berlin, and other European capitals. The limited opportunities in the then small town were stifling to the ambitious youth; but he made the best of his leisure hours in study and reading.

Then one noon a bell-hop interrupted his playing. He was wanted on an urgent long distance call. The voice on the other end was that of the Manager of the Boston Symphony Orchestra. There was an opening in the second violin section for the coming 1915-1916 season. Would he take it? Arthur accepted with relief and enthusiasm.

In Symphony Hall his father's old friends extended cordial hands. Arthur Fiedler, at twenty, was the youngest member of the group who responded to the baton of Karl Muck. The former conductor of the Royal Opera of Berlin had returned to Boston in 1912, after spending four years back in Berlin. This time he came with special permission from the Kaiser, who ranked the Boston Symphony with the best in Europe.

Muck readily accepted this pupil of the musicians he had known in his Berlin years. He remembered Arthur, too, as the bright lad who sometimes had come to rehearsals with his father during his first two-year tenure as Boston Symphony conductor in 1906-1908.

Even at twelve Arthur Fiedler's ebullience had made his presence felt. He had still been the "quiet boy" described by his sisters; yet, his responsive smile reflected the security that dwells in the heart of one who knows that he is loved.

Probably no words had passed between them in those earlier years. But now the expressive eyes of this son of the Boston Symphony fastened on the slight conductor, and some inner communication bound Arthur Fiedler to Karl Muck. The strict discipline of this perfectionist brought Emanuel's precepts into focus again. Arthur was not unprepared for the Muck regime. Willy Hess had often described his experiences as concert master under the man who had "given a living voice to the perfect instrument left by Gericke." Arthur poured devotion into the tone of the violin which now blended into that voice. He gave alert attention to the conducting skill of the Prussian master. It did not take the Maestro long to discover the versatility of the young man who could easily slip onto the piano or organ bench when needed, or fill in if a violist were absent. In fact, Arthur's proficiency and love of that instrument soon brought him a transfer to the viola section.

It was as a violist that Arthur Fiedler participated in the first recording ever made by a symphony orchestra in America when the Boston Symphony went to Camden, New Jersey in 1917. The players were crammed into two wooden igloos, like the halves of oranges not quite put together. The strings were all crowded into one; winds, brasses, and percussion in the other. The conductor sat on a stool in the middle.

Two large horns picked up the sound at the openings, and the recordings were pressed on wax. Wax impressions made from the master were achieved by weights because electricity was not yet trusted. Each disc could record only four minutes and forty seconds, and it had to be exacly right in one recording—no splicing of tape in those days! Each time the bassoon fumbled in a treacherous spot the sweltering players had to start over again, and stay with it until the four-minute-forty second piece was perfect.

Over forty years later Fiedler was rummaging through a second-hand record shop in New York with Martin Bookspan of Station WQXR when he came upon a set of these old recordings "in mint condition." He purchased these reminders of his youthful experience for twenty-five cents per record and took them home to treasure among his most valued possessions.

There had been no more such recordings in those

ill-omened months of 1917. Viola playing became suddenly unimportant as America took up the Allied battle
cry. The Boston Symphony Orchestra was rapidly being
divested of its younger members when Arthur answered
the call for Navy enlistement. But the man who has
become familiar to world audiences as a broad-shoul-
dered, firmly-built conductor, springing up steps to podiums in his seventies with the vigor and enthusiasm of
youth, was turned down as "too short and too thin!" He
stuffed on bananas and drank all the water he could
hold; but he was rebuffed by the Army and again by
the Air Force.

Then the draft caught him. Panic had seized the
nation as news from the war zone worsened. Marshall
Foch messaged President Wilson that "there is danger
of the war being lost unless the numerical inferiority of
the Allies can be remedied as rapidly as possible by the
advent of American troops."

The examining doctor looked Arthur over hur-
riedly. "Those feet are not very good," he admitted,
"but we'll take you anyway."

Arthur sold the furnishings of his small flat, sent
his dog, "Muzzi," to a friend in New Hampshire, and
marched off to Camp Devens. Like every rookie, he was
assigned menial tasks. One morning as he was sweeping
up the horse barn, he heard a familiar "ta-ta-ta-taa"
whistle. These first four notes of Beethoven's Fifth Symphony had become the traditional recognition signal of
Symphony Hall associates. Looking down from the loft

was Leslie Rogers, Librarian of the Boston Symphony!

Rogers' "ha-ha-ha" was not as hard to take as the unaccustomed routine and the "terrible food." Release came unexpectedly two weeks later when Arthur was called in for physical re-check.

"Who the hell sent you here?" demanded the scornful officer. "Look at those feet! The flattest I ever saw. Get out."

Arthur came back to a Boston suspicious of anyone with a Teutonic name. German musicians who had neglected naturalization were being summarily dismissed. Fortunately, Uncle Bernard had survived. Good violists were rare. Young Fiedler was welcomed back.

Hysterical rumors were centering around Karl Muck. He was accused of sending secret radio information to his patron, the Kaiser. Then some Providence patriots set a trap. En route back from a concert which he had conducted in the Rhode Island capital, he read the morning paper. The Editor had called him a "no good German, who had refused to play *The Star Spangled Banner.*"

"But nobody told me they wanted it!" Muck turned to his concert master, dismayed. "If I had known, I certainly would have played it."

Investigation showed that the request had gone to the management, who had referred it to Colonel Higginson, founder and long-time President of the Trustees of the Boston Symphony Orchestra. But he had seen no need of beginning a symphony with a patriotic anthem.

The request had never reached Muck. Next, Pittsburgh refused to have Muck conduct in that city.

Other complaints were brought against the Conductor. Arthur was at rehearsal when Federal officers walked into Symphony Hall to arrest the eminent musician. The result was that Muck spent the remainder of the war in an internment camp.

Summer vacation in 1918 was a trying period for young Fiedler. With Waldo Mayo, concert violinist who later became musical director for the popular Major Bowes' radio orchestra, he rented a bungalow at Rockport—then an inconspicuous beach resort not yet taken over by its "Artists' Colony." They decorated their small dwelling with gay Japanese lanterns and sat in the evenings watching the white-capped Atlantic. What was innocent pleasure to them was misinterpreted by hysterical neighbors. Prying officials came to search every corner of the house, looking for receiving sets for messages from U-boats which had been spotted off the Massachusetts coast.

Five miles away numbers of Gloucester fishing boats were frequently sunk by these U-boats. Natives were justifiably suspicious when two apparently healthy young men, not in the Army, spent their days "fiddling" and lighted vari-colored lanterns each evening. Fiedler and Mayo—both 4-F—did not advertise the fact that they were preparing for a concert tour with the famous tenor, Enrico Caruso. The day that the two tucked violins into cases and left suddenly caused consternation in the town. Rockport residents, feeling that the coast was about to be shelled after the suspects had safely left the scene of impending disaster, took to their cellars. Arthur and Waldo climbed onto the train, en route to Saratoga Springs, New York, where their first concert with Caruso was scheduled—entirely unaware of the excitement they had left behind.

Caruso's trunks were being unloaded at the United States Hotel in Saratoga Springs just as the young violinists arrived. Their curiosity whetted by a large wicker basket, they asked the singer's baggage-master what it contained. They learned that Caruso always traveled with six large down pillows, the fulfillment of a dream of a poor Neapolitan street singer who had vowed that if he ever became famous and rich he would sleep on such pillows for the rest of his life.

Their relations with this Metropolitan tenor began cordially. The young men were practicing on stage the morning of the concert when Caruso, his accompanist, and his entire entourage arrived—also for rehearsal. Hastily the boys stopped playing in deference to the famous older man; but Caruso seated himself in the front of the stage and graciously urged them to finish their numbers.

Fiedler and Mayo discovered that their function in this concert was to give the great man a chance to rest between his own vocal numbers. While he was on stage they watched two faithful valets standing nervously in the wings. One held a peeled apple; the other, a lighted cigarette, on either of which the tenor could vent his wrath if he "broke" on a high note.

The concert tour completed, the two "suspects" returned to "Pagan Villa," their Rockport retreat, to a chorus of children following them from the train, shouting, "there are the spies back again." And they opened their groceries to discover that the special rye bread ordered for them from Boston was punctured with holes because the grocer had been warned that coded messages might be hidden under its crusts.

CHAPTER THREE

A Baton of His Own

STATELY HENRY RABAUD, be-whiskered Parisian conductor, motioned the post-Armistice audience to rise as Arthur Fiedler at the great organ filled Symphony Hall with the swelling strains of *The Star Spangled Banner*. The wartime custom had become a tradition for this mentor of American Symphony Orchestras. In addition to his post in the violas, Fiedler was by now the regular pianist and organist. His versatility was making him indispensable, for he could just as easily shift to the violins if strengthening there was necessary, or he could play the celesta when the score called for that rare instrument. His associates referred jestingly to him as the "floating kidney of the orchestra."

Outside of Symphony Hall he was earning a sobriquet of quite another sort. His nimble fingers and instinctive accord as an accompanist soon brought him to the drawing rooms of Back Bay homes with the frequency of his former Berlin engagements. Visiting artists appearing in smaller concert series at Jordan Hall or in the assembly halls of nearby colleges usually sought young Fiedler to accompany them. "Boston's most popular bachelor" was finding life full and exciting. In fact, the girls became so enamoured of the captivating pianist that at one time the Conservatory forbade his flirtatious intrusion. This did not deeply trouble him. At heart he was serious, concerned not with frippery girls, but with a driving ambition to fulfill the potentialities recognized nearly ten years ago by his professors of conducting, Arno Kleffel and Rudolph Krasselt.

With the opening of the 1919-1920 season, stimulus came with the arrival of Pierre Monteux. The new conductor, who had had to complete a contract with the Metropolitan Opera before he could accept the Boston position, brought *joie de vivre* into the staid city. Arthur played with zest when Monteux introduced the music of Debussy and Stravinsky, stirring his audiences with musical excursions into freshly-creative fields.

Fiedler discovered that the sturdy Maestro had once been a viola player himself; that he had risen through the ranks to the conductor's post. Monteux had first conducted small string ensembles, going from that to the direction of ballet, opera, and symphony orchestras all over Europe. America had responded to his art when he toured the United States with the Ballet Russe and had kept him on at the Metropolitan, Each week, as Arthur learned more about this Maestro, he was spurred to emulate that musical career. If Monteux could do all this, why not Fiedler?

Their relationship suffered severe strain early in the season. Monteux had been in conflict with Concert Master Fradkin over the issue of unionization. Matters came to a head behind the scenes before a Friday afternoon concert. Fradkin refused to stand at the Maestro's signal. Nearly half the orchestra sided with the concert master. Others vacillated. As the pro-union members lined up on one side of the room, the undecided moved back and forth. Arthur, young and excitable, cast his lot with the strikers. Then he watched from the wings as stubborn Monteux led about forty-five non-striking musicians onto the stage to give a disappointed audience an abbreviated concert.

Arthur's night was restless. The next morning he woke, contrite. In all his thinking the audience has had prior consideration. "Those people were entitled to the concert they had paid to hear," he reasoned.

Monday morning he called the management. "I am ashamed," he admitted. "I'd like to be re-instated."

As the doughty Frenchman re-built his orchestra, Arthur Fiedler was the only striker taken back, thus preserving the continuity of his association with the Boston Symphony organization from 1915.

That season of 1919-1920 there were three Fiedlers in the orchestra. Uncle Benny had remained loyal through the strife. Uncle Gus was hired to replace a recalcitrant violinist. Arthur's admiration and friendship for Monteux increased. He began in earnest to pattern his career on that of Monteux.

The first step was to organize a "Fiedler Trio," differing in personnel and instruments from the family group of Berlin days. Instead of a pianist, he enlisted the Boston Symphony's solo harpist, Alfred Holy. This graduate of Prague Conservatory, a native of Portugal, had played with some of the great orchestras of Europe. Jacobus Langendoen, newly appointed to the 'cello section of the Boston Symphony after Monteux had listened to him briefly in The Hague the previous summer, completed the Trio.

The two young men, Langendoen and Fiedler, were to be congenial throughout long careers with the organization which first brought them together. Their enthusiasm, combined with the mature harpist whose experience had included playing at Bayreuth Festivals, made this trio welcome at chamber music concerts in and around Boston. Their tours were not always pleasure trips. One midwinter night with snow swirling in great gusts they started off for Mt. Holyoke College in a battered old taxicab, the best a penny-pinching manager would provide. The driver and a pal occupied the front seat. In the back the three musicians, plus violin and 'cello, huddled to keep warm as snow blew in through leaky, half-shut doors. (The harp had been shipped ahead.) Before they left Boston the car's radiator was steaming, but the driver did some tinkering and they kept going, arriving too late for food. Committee ladies hustled coffee and sandwiches from a nearby drugstore, and numbed fingers were thawed enough to delight the audience with numbers performed as smoothly as if they had traveled in cushioned luxury. Then the old cab chugged up to take them on the long trip back. Mid-way they were stopped by State Troopers who poked flashlights into the crowded back seat, inquiring suspiciously, "What's that?" as Langendoen hugged the massive 'cello protectively. His friendly wave satisfied the officers, and they were on their way again, swearing vengeance on a manager who thought so little of his clients' comfort.

Arthur, well indoctrinated by his early musical tours in Europe, was undaunted by discomfort. By 1924 he had the Boston Sinfonietta on the road—twenty-one picked players from the parent organization. Boston's acceptance of Monteux straying from traditional program-making encouraged Fiedler to share some of the unusual chamber music he had enjoyed in Berlin. His "small, expert, and polished orchestra" played for the Harvard Musical Association and opened the 1927-1928 concert series at Wheaton College in Norton. Although Wagner was not yet completely acceptable to conservative Bostonians, Fiedler's Sinfonietta carried his audience through the moods of the *Siegfried Idyll* as they seemed to hear birds in the dark forest and waterfalls gushing out of craggy Bavarian Alps.

The Symphony Hall debut of the group brought Boston's leading musical families to listen to this conductor whose talents were being devoted to furthering the cause of better music in the jazz age. Among the patrons on that auspicious night were Governor and Mrs. Alvan T. Fuller, whose sponsorship would have a determining influence on all of Arthur Fiedler's future.

As Viola Davenport, the Governor's wife had been recognized among Boston's finest concert singers, and had often appeared as a member of the Boston Opera casts. After her marriage she gave up her professionl career, but her clear bell-like soprano continued to delight audiences at benefits and smaller concerts. Wherever she appeared, with Arthur Fiedler's sensitive fingers responding to her every nuance, applause expressed the love of Boston's music devotees. Her husband, proud of his talented wife, lent more than "name" support to the versatile accompanist.

Within a few years the confidence of the Governor would help Arthur Fiedler revolutionize Boston's musical habits; and a vivacious little girl who ran in and out of the adjoining hallway while "Aunt Ollie" was rehearsing with the handsome accompanist would grow up to change the ways of Boston's gregarious and popular bachelor.

But in the mid-twenties his professional card proclaimed Arthur Fiedler merely as "Vocal Coach and Accompanist, 270 Huntington Avenue, Boston, Mass." A morning rehearsal in this apartment with his pal from Rockport brought them both an unexpected friendship. It was warm and the two rehearsed with open windows.

Intensely preoccupied with the music, it took them some time to notice two young blond girls leaning over their window sill in the house across the street, apparently entranced with the free concert. The adventurous young men wasted no time in making contact, discovering that their admirers were actresses rehearsing for a play in a downtown theatre. Exchange of complimentary tickets to their respective performances brought a surprise to Fiedler and Mayo, who had thought somewhat condescendingly that their new acquaintances were chorus girls. When they arrived at the theatre they read the program and realized that they were to see leading lady Jeanne Eagels and Catherine Haydn, a featured actress playing opposite George Arliss in "Lady Hamilton."

From then on Jeanne Eagels was part of their circle of treasured friends. They listened concernedly to her ambitions to become a great actress, chiding her for mainly playing ingenue roles without much dramatic substance. Some years went by without contact and then all three were in Paris at the same time. Miss Eagels brought them the manuscript of a new play which had been offered her, insisting that at last she had a part that would satisfy her ambition. Her Boston friends were shocked to find that she was to assay the role of prostitute and could not enthuse about their sweet young Jeanne as such a heavy character. But they had to retract their objections some time later when they read of the phenomenal success she scored in "Rain."

Jeanne Eagels was only one of many aspiring young

artists who appreciated Arthur's musical and artistic abilities. When critics reviewed concerts of 'cellists, violinists, and singers they often gave enthusiastic lines to the man at the piano. "He accompanied admirably, that is to say, with intelligence," they would write . . . "he played with customary skill, taste, and sympathetic insight" . . . "Bedetti first 'cellist of the Boston Symphony) shared the concert with Arthur Fiedler's expert and reciprocating accompaniment . . ."

Impressario M. A. Margolis was so impressed by these continuing notices that he engaged the young man to accompany all future visiting artists under his management. During this period the Sinfonietta was also gaining in number and reputation, not only in Boston, but in other New England cities. Sister Elsa, now married, had returned to America and was living in New York. She often toured with the group as solo pianist.

Fan letters began to reward Fiedler for daring to include such innovators as Schönberg, Stravinsky, Honegger, and Hindemith. "I hope," wrote a Harvard enthusiast, "that this is only the beginning of other concerts which will help to relieve some of the starvation for present-day music outside the Symphony program."

All of his fans were not in college halls or drawing rooms. The Boston acquaintanceship widened nightly just as in Berlin. Exhilarated after a concert, he would roam the streets, sometimes alone, more often with a congenial friend. Jazz bands in night clubs or the guitars of Portuguese fishermen along the wharves intrigued him.

He joined in with Italian "Caro Mio." Sometimes he danced a jig with the Irish. He talked with Negroes about their Voodoo drums. He sensed a "starvation" more acute than this Harvard correspondent had inferred. People of all classes in Boston hungered for good music. He would feed them!

This thought percolated through all his planning as the long Boston Symphony playing season came to a close. He enjoyed the change of pace provided by the Spring Pops which his father's friend, Wilhelm Gericke, had instituted as early as 1885 to give his men longer months of employment and to keep them in top form after the winter series was over. But he knew that even the cheapest balcony seats for the Pops were beyond the resources of the music-hungry people of his night acquaintance. He carried these people on his mind when June ended and it was time for his annual visit to the family overseas. Ever since war had forced separation from them he had assumed their main support through years of privation incident to that conflict and its aftermath. As soon as peace returned he had managed every summer to get back to Europe, even if it meant shoveling coal on a freighter.

One of these summers Arthur and his friend, Waldo Mayo, received an invitation from an executive of the William Steamship Company to sail on a freighter plying between Norfolk, Virginia, and Rotterdam. They accepted, anticipating a seventeen-day voyage to be divided between sunning on deck and practicing. But they

arrived in Norfolk just as a shipping strike was called
and their vacation was postponed for three weeks. Invitations from the country club set offered some respite
from tedium. Then they discovered the enlivening music
of the colored section. A city ordinance decreed this off
limits to whites, with a penalty of a ten dollar fine or two
days in jail. The Boston musicians defied the law, which
apparently was not very rigorously enforced, and spent
evenings as musically exciting and stimulating as any
either had ever experienced. Soon they were joining in
the contagious crescendo of the incessant rhythm in a
frenzy of hand clapping, shouting, and singing. Each café
had its own band and singers with intermittent contests.
This native jazz, new to the northerners, was as heady as
May wine. They were carried away with it, exhilarated
as much as they were later in Paris when they first heard
Stravinsky's *Sacre du Printemps*.

At last the strike was over. Their little piano was
hoisted onto the deck of the *S.S. Conshohocken*. Nights
were spent with the crew—men of every conceivable na-
tionality—swapping stories and shooting dice. The Japanese stewards's "Blekfast ready" at seven each morning
was an unwelcome call. Fiedler's consistent winning
streak soon turned the crew's friendliness into stony, sullen silence as they saw their wages disappearing into the
musician's wallet. His friend urged him to try to lose,
to no avail, until about two days from the end of the
voyage. Then he lost all his gains and more. They landed

safely and celebrated with the crew all the first day along the shorefront pubs of Rotterdam.

Before joining his family in Berlin, Arthur and his pal spent some time at a North Sea resort. The German mark was fast depreciating and they carried their huge bundle of paper money in a large ebony and ivory box which Mayo tucked under his arm. The government printing press could hardly keep pace with the rapidly falling mark on the exchange. Yesterday's 1000 mark bills were merely crossed out and 10,000 substituted. Soon a million mark bill was reprinted as 500 million and then one billion. The print was so fresh that fingers were smeared in handling the paper.

A billboard on the leading boardwalk café intrigued the two Americans into an international "Nikolashka" drinking contest. Nikolashka is a liquer glass of brandy topped off with a slice of lemon. The drinker pours a quarter teaspoon of sugar into the center of the lemon, folds the lemon in half, bites it, leaving the ring, and washes it down with the brandy in one gulp. Many tables displayed flags of the teams—hefty Swedes and Germans, Czechs, Viennese, Hungarians and many others. The American travelers looked dubiously at the little Stars and Stripes on their table, wondering if they could possibly uphold the honor of their country against such strong competition. They never considered themselves a match for heavy drinkers.

The night passed, leaving a total memory blank;

but sometime in the early morning hours they came to
as a cheering crowd was throwing napkins at them. They
faced a table littered with empty brandy bottles, a stack
of lemon slices, a nearly empty sugar bowl, and a basket
of rolls. Cheering turned to angry cries of *"der verdamte
Amerikan"* when the victorious pair playfully tossed the
rolls at the crowd. The painful memory of the famine
years turned their bread wasting into an unpardonable
insult and they were hustled into the street in disgrace.

Booted out of the North Sea resort, they entrained
in another direction, ending their vacation with a walking trip through the Black Forest. Knapsacks on back,
they trudged through the rough terrain, shaded by slender firs. At the end of the week they caught a train to
Weisbaden. Mayo's bloody attempt to shave off his beard
with a razor in the men's room while the train lurched
along bumpy ties brought nothing but derisive laughter
from Arthur. Nevertheless, they walked up the carpeted
steps of the leading Weisbaden Hotel, ignoring the
posted sign requiring "formal dress" in honor of a visiting monarch, and requested rooms for the night. The
astonished clerk looked hesitantly at his dirty, bearded,
and bloody applicants, and then, apparently taking them
for rich *"Verückte Amerikaner"* assigned them a place
to sleep. Relaxation and well being returned the next
morning when they visited the famous Roman baths and
were unexpectedly taken in hand by two giant masseurs
who kneaded their tired muscles from head to toe.

Arthur was now ready for his family visit in Berlin, and happy hours in the Tiergarten sipping beer and listening to symphonies with his father, mother, and 'Rika, sometimes joined by Rosa and her husband, Morris Hochland. Plenty of pretty fräuleins, too, were ready to dance under the stars with the graceful young American. Other summers, if he stopped off in Vienna to see the old grandparents, he always found time for a Strauss evening in the Stadtpark. Or there might be a garden concert in Schönbrunn, where the fragrance of roses on the night air mingled with the perfume of some Viennese beauty clinging to his arm.

Always he came back to Boston wishing that he could bring some of this atmosphere with him. One late summer night in the 'twenties he was strolling along the bank of the Charles River. Sunset lit rosy clouds above the white columns of M.I.T. on the opposite bank. Sail boats floated lazily in the afterglow. This was it! Like the little boy bursting to tell his family about the night with Buffalo Bill's Indians, he hastened to share his plans with the Fullers.

"Arthur, you're insane!" protested the former Governor. But he listened as Arthur described the motley crowd who would gladly spend summer evenings on the grassy Esplanade listening to the world's greatest music, free to everyone. And all this, insisted the excited young man, would be underwritten by public subscription.

"It can't be done!" with this ejaculation Fuller tried to stem the tide of words. "July weather is bad. The place is bad. There'd be hoodlums and pickpockets . . .

but," his tone changing as he looked into Arthur's plead-
ing eyes. "If you can persuade ten other people to give a
thousand each, I'll double it!"

That was all Arthur needed. Now he would and
could succeed.

"There are so many music-lovers in Boston who
cannot afford even fifty cents for a top balcony seat . . .
we are not going to play only light music . . . just regular
Symphony pieces for those who remember them from
their childhood in the Old Country . . . for the children
who are growing up without the right musical memories. . . ." Thus he insisted whenever his knock was answered. Many a door was shut in his face; but the Fuller
name and his own indomitable belief in what he wanted
finally won out.

On the night of July 4, 1929, Arthur Fiedler stood
on a platform inside a wooden structure shaped like a
quarter of a baseball, called an "acoustic shell," not a
*band*stand. The Metropolitan District Commission, impressed by the financial support of the small group of
public-spirited citizens who had responded to Fiedler's
pleas, had erected this shell on grounds subject to their
jurisdiction.

Thirty years later Fiedler described the event and
his emotions. . . . "In front of me sat forty-six musicians.
They looked out on a crowd which partly stood, and
partly sat in folding chairs. I was about to start the
Esplanade Concerts, first series of open air concerts
known to Boston. They were to be offered free to the

public through the philanthropy of a small group whom I had persuaded to back the idea after a personal campaign of several years.

"Appropriately for the evening of Independence Day, I opened with Sousa's *The Stars and Stripes Forever*. It turned out that I was also opening what was musically the worst fiasco of my career. The acoustic shell had been built from a scale model which had seemed satisfactory from experimenting with it by ringing a small bell inside it. But at every succeeding bar of Sousa's great march I was hearing the most unexpected sound effects. I had wanted to show how much richer the march sounded with the addition of strings than it did just with band instruments. But the sound of the strings was not getting out front. The bass tuba and piccolo were really outstanding. So was the bass drum—which, in fact, after every boom was followed by several delayed echoes straggling into measures where they did not belong.

"Suddenly the breezes from the river whirled into the shell and came out with sheets of music which had not been clipped to the stands. Men, women, boys picked them up and laid them at the front of the stage, from where they were relayed to their owners, who, meanwhile, had kept on playing by looking at someone else's music."

Fiedler was almost afraid to open the papers the next morning. He was lucky. The accounts had not been written by music critics; but rather, by sharp-eyed news reporters, who described the large, interested and well-behaved crowd and predicted that these free orchestral concerts, led and played by Boston Symphony musicians should "prove to be a great summer attraction."

Fiedler was determined that his interested audience should hear the music as it should be interpreted. He took his sound problems to Dr. William R. Barss, Head of the Acoustics Laboratory at the Massachusetts Institute of Technology across the river. The expert listened attentively to Fiedler's account. Then he made a pencilled sketch. "The troubles are caused," he said, "by the angle at which the shell faces the walls of buildings in the distance, and also by failure to notice the live and less live spots inside the shell. Change the seating of your musicians according to this sketch, and I'll gamble there will be an improvement. While this is being tried, I'll listen and suggest any possible further changes."

The orchestra was literally "turned inside out," with the strings all seated in the center of the shell, as Dr. Barss and the conductor combined their skills to provide the best possible effect for the thousands who sat on the grass—or rented folding chairs at ten cents each—nearly every night for the five weeks after that opening concert. All ages and classes were there, and as one commentator described the scene, "The old Italian woman who carries her own chair for a mile to save a dime and a woman in a limousine had the same expression when the strains of *Liebestraum* floated on the night air."

Even rain did not change the schedule. One night

Gaston Elcus, concert master of the Esplanade orchestra, played the Bach-Gounod *Ave Maria* while over a thousand people stood in a drenching downpour. A reviewer wrote that a "symphony of thunder roared across the sky and blazing lightning lit the dramatic scene in weird fashion as Elcus fought the elements to render with exquisite beauty the solo which was the *piece de resistance* of the program.

"His precious violin is worth more than $3,000, yet he stood in pelting rain with bared head, lost in the beauty of the composition and actually making the listeners stay on despite the storm. During the presentation he mopped the violin with his handkerchief, had another musician tightening the pegs as water loosened strings, and during an orchestral interval dashed for the musician's shelter to mop off the Guillaume violin with chamois, so that the number could be finished. . . ."

People who had started to stampede out as the waves of the turbulent river smashed against the shore had been held spellbound as "the wordless prayer of the violin rose clear and strong above the rumble of thunder. By twos and threes they crowded close to the shell, newspapers over their heads, and listened to the end. Then, scarcely waiting to applaud, they dashed away, the musicians wiped their instruments and packed them into cases. The concert was over."

Another night a sudden squall threatened the precious strings. Immediately the horns moved forward to make a human screen, playing on with backs to the audience and the rain! Rather than risk more danger to his instruments on a night when five hundred early comers were stretched on the grass as the heavens opened, Fiedler sent an announcer to say that the concert would be canceled.

"We'll stay if you'll play," one enthusiast shouted, and the crowd took up the chant. The Maestro decided to bow to their demand, and was rewarded. The rain ceased as quickly as it had begun.

Rain was not the only hazard. There were hot nights when the woodwind players found themselves munching mosquitoes. Other insects attracted by the lights swarmed and buzzed in annoying obbligatos.

Sometimes, despite Dr. Barss' helpful suggestions, the wooden shell played acoustical tricks. Resounding chords reflected back, or words spoken *sotto voce* were magnified to an unintended audience. A flute player announcing an encore was stuck by the German text.

"Oh hell!" he whispered, "I don't know *what* it is," and the freakish shell re-echoed *magne voce* to a delighted audience.

Again, comments on the lawn would be pulled back into the shell, and the amused players heard a sympathetic listener say, "I don't see why those musicians play for him. I understand he doesn't even pay them."

It was not only smashed mosquitoes which ran up the cleaner bills for those white-coated players. One grateful elderly patron, who always danced when the

Blue Danube filled the summer air, arrived early and put a chocolate bar on every musician's seat. The night was hot and muggy. Her gifts were appreciated only by the dry cleaning shops the following morning.

"No Peddlers" signs helped preserve quiet for the attentive audience. Possibly the feared hoodlums and pickpockets came under the spell. The music critic of a New York paper joined the listeners to comment on "perhaps the most cosmopolitan assemblage ever seen in Boston . . . where the light police force had little to do but stand with folded arms and listen."

One man, obviously a hobo, stood every night under the same tree on the outskirts of the crowd. He spoke to no one, but his face showed contentment in contrast to his shabby clothes. A dowager rustled into her rented chair and began to make learned comments on the music. A tap on her shoulder and she turned to face an old lady in a tattered shawl.

"Y'ain't supposed to talk when they're playing," the woman whispered.

And so Bostonians came to know one another as the evening star shone in the twilight sky and the strains of Tannhäuser floated up to listeners in Beacon Street's open windows.

When Governor Allen spoke at the final performance of the first season—on August 18, 1929—he thanked the public-spirited citizens who had financed this great experiment, and the Metropolitan Park Commission for the shell. He promised that The Esplanade Concerts would be an important part of the Boston Tercentenary to be held the following year.

Success in the first season of his dream-come-true brought new opportunity. In November, 1929, the Conductor of The Esplanade Concerts presided over the rebirth of The Cecilia Society. The appointment of Arthur Fiedler to lead this organization, which antedated the Boston Symphony Orchestra by four years, was hailed with eclat. "He is young, able, with a personal and increasing following. His forces respond to him; he interests audiences. There is no questioning his musical intelligence and open-mindedness. Now deserved opportunity opens for him . . . again, The Cecilia has a future!"

Now "the Poo-Bah of the Boston Symphony Orchestra" had another service to render in the winter series. Serge Koussevitzky, who had replaced Monteux five years earlier, had been using the Harvard-Radcliffe Chorus to carry the vocal parts of classical oratorios. As he programmed the coming season he included Debussy's music to D'Annunzio's *The Martyrdom of Saint Sebastian.* He turned to his young violist. Could he train The Cecilia to present this difficult music, to him, Debussy's crowning achievement?

The January "Notice to Prospects" for the Cecilia Society urged new singers to grasp the "opportunity of being trained by Arthur Fiedler, who is without question the best man for this work in the country. . . . Probably there is no other chorus in this or any other part of the

country that can undertake the class of music we are
given to sing."

Arthur recalled the days when The Cecilia had
ranked with the Kneisel Quartet in making musical history. His father and the indefatigable B. J. Lang, The
Cecilia's founder, had been good friends. He had heard
Emanuel describe the use Nikisch had made of these
singers in choral-symphony combinations. He was determined to make himself and his chorus equally valuable
to Koussevitzky.

He was a finicky, exacting choir master, directing
his group with precision. The day came when he was
ready to place them under the Maestro's baton for a first
orchestra-chorus rehearsal. The stern Russian-born,
French-adopted Koussevitzky directed with what became
known as "musical shorthand." He expected his players
to sense the omitted strokes. The Cecilians were confused.

"I thought you said they were ready," he snapped
at Fiedler.

"They don't understand your beat," he answered
courteously. "May I show you?"

Koussevitzky acquiesced.

"So," he said in his halting English. "I take lessons
from ze young!"

Voices blended in perfect rhythm, as their leader's
baton marked each measure.

"So," Koussevitzy acknowledged success. "But my
way saves energy."

Success with The Cecilia enhanced Fiedler's repu-

tation among Boston's musical elite; but it was The Esplanade that was winning the hearts of the people. When
the second season of the outdoor concerts opened in July,
Judge Frederick Cabot, President of the Trustees, praised
Arthur Fiedler "who has brought the people of Boston
together in a common spiritual union. It has taken Boston 299 years to bring this about. Let its 300th birthday
mark permanent establishment of the concerts as an integral part of Boston life."

By the thousands people thronged from all over
Greater Boston to give assent. Fiedler overheard a re-
mark that listening to music in the setting of The Esplanade made a person "feel like a millionaire." He esti-
mated that as this second season progressed, he had about
50,000 "millionaires" saying thank you by their continuing attendance.

Donors mingled inconspicuously among the shab-
bily dressed loungers on the grass, keeping their own
garb informal enough to hide their identity. One of the
largest donors lent a match to a fellow listener.

"Like the music?" the recipient inquired.

"Sort of," said the older man.

"Sort of!" the young man was indignant. "Why,
even if I paid, I'd think I was getting more than my
money's worth."

"Well, I don't know. That's about how I feel,"
replied the incognito real millionaire.

"Glad you're not the crumb I took you for!" whispered the booster as Arthur Fiedler bounced up the steps to conduct the next number.

"I've given money for all sorts of things," the patron commented as he told this story later, "but I never got more satisfaction than for these Esplanade concerts. These are the most astonishing assemblages ever gathered in Boston—the most thoroughly cosmopolitan, quietest, most mutually respectful mixtures of people. What an adventure for donors to listen to comments re 'the rich guys that won't let on who they are.'"

If it was an adventure for the donors, it gave perhaps even more pleasure to the thousands of listeners in the wide basin where the lights of Cambridge on the opposite shore were reflected in the river. This grassy plot at the foot of Mt. Vernon Street on the Boston side where the Charles basin makes an angle is easy of access to the congested West End and to Beacon Hill. Foreign-born from the North End mingled with students from summer schools, members of old families from Newton and Cambridge, and business men kept in town during the hot summer while their wives and children vacationed on Cape Cod. Music was a common denominator. The fact that tastes are basically similar was demonstrated in the All-request program given on August 1. *"Pomp and Circumstance*—thereafter a Fiedler favorite in opening concerts all over the world—was followed by the *Peer Gynt Suite, Tannhaüser, Kammenoi Ostrow,* Handel's *Largo,* the *Blue Danube Waltzes.*

As the season closed with 25,000 people in the audience on August 20th, The Esplanade Concerts were firmly established as an indispensable feature of Boston life. Clamor to hear more from Arthur Fiedler rose in chorus from every section of the city.

CHAPTER FOUR

❦

"Popular Music Is Familiar Music"

In the spring of that same year—1930—Arthur Fiedler became the eighteenth conductor of the Boston Pops Orchestra—the first Boston-born musician to lift a baton over that group. He had played under six of the former conductors, while between his father and Uncle Benny there had always been Fiedlers in the organization. He came to the task prepared not only by training and experience, but also with deeply ingrained memories of The Pops' original purpose and success.

As a very small boy he had been allowed to go with his mother and sisters to watch Papa and Uncle play at the pioneer Pops, which Gericke had patterned after the Bilse concerts in Berlin. Later, in his student days at the Royal Academy, those concerts had become familiar.

Recent changes in the character of the Boston Pops under Jacchia and Casella, with their seemingly conde-

scending attitude about what they termed "popular"
music, had disturbed him. He liked to think of the men
and women he remembered, riding up to Symphony Hall
on their old-fashioned bicycles to sit around bare tables
sipping lemonade just flavored with claret while their
feet tapped in rhythm to gay mazurkas. He sensed that
just as crocuses burst out of the frozen ground and deco-
rators transformed the staid hall from its winter formality to a semblance of a Venetian garden or a Schönbrun,
so the audience of the 'thirties wanted to refresh their
spirits with lilting melodies.

Twice during his years with the Symphony he had
had opportunity to test his powers with such audiences.
Four years earlier, Jacchia, in a pique over a cut in the
size of the orchestra, had refused to conduct the closing
concert. The fiery Italian accused Koussevitzky of jeal-
ousy over the success of the Pops and resigned with a
threat that he would return to Boston the following year
to found a competing Pops.

"I re-created the Pops after the war," he told the
press. "Only since then have these concerts become popular from a musical viewpoint. Previously, they were only
drinking parties. I refuse to be present to take part in
the burial."

That closing concert, on July 3, 1926, had proved
to be anything but a "burial." When thirty-two-year-old
Fiedler, selected to fill the vacancy, had stepped to the
podium to lead Sousa's stirring *The Stars and Stripes Forever* each player responded with verve. A large audience

who had come mainly out of curiosity to see what a daring young man would do in the place of the experienced Agide Jacchia, put down their glasses to clap vociferously. But the real test came with the next number—von Weber's *Overture to Oberon.* In spite of slight nervousness when the youthful conductor bowed, orchestra and audience were soon under a spell. Cheers, which first sounded out of friendliness, now acclaimed skillful musicianship.

Station WEEI made it possible for a far-flung radio audience to catch the enthusiasm as the program ran the gamut from a Liszt *Hungarian Rhapsody* and Kreisler's *Liebesfreud* to Sullivan's *Lost Chord* and *Auld Lang Syne.* "The Boston Advertiser" summed up the triumph by saying, "A Boston boy fought a battle against odds at Symphony Hall last night and won—hands down—with *The Lost Chord."*

In spite of the reviews that acclaimed his "auspicious premier" as Pops' conductor, and noted his "sensitive regard for musical structure, his keen rhythmic sense and impeccable taste," the time had not yet come for Arthur Fiedler to assume the title which would eventually bring him international renown. Alfred Casella was appointed the next regular conductor of the Boston Pops Orchestra.

Arthur Fiedler had returned to the viola section and to his continuing engagements with the Trio and The Sinfonietta—except for one brilliant night in 1928. Serious Casella had refused to conduct when the noisy

audience, assembled for "Al Smith Nite," offended his
ego. The management argued in vain. It was time for the
orchestra to take their places. Instinctively, they looked
to Arthur Fiedler, edging toward the Manager. "If you
wish, I'll take over," he volunteered. Before the evening
was over, he had the gay audience singing *Sidewalks of
New York, Will You Love Me in December,* and *Victory
Parade.*

The Victory proved to be Fiedler's rather than
Smith's; but it took two more years to consummate it. In
the interim the musician whom Jacchia had once threatened to fire as an "incorrigible" continued to build a
warm place in the affection of Boston's public. Doting
mammas exposed their daughters to his charm at soirees
after Sinfonietta concerts. Younger singers clamored for
places in The Cecilia. Society editors vied with music
critics in mentioning the debonair musician who seemed
to be on every important invitation list.

With unflagging energy he sped from studio to
salon, from podium to theatre. He even played the part
of Maurice in *Fallen Angels* "in a truly Gallic manner"
when the Little Theatre Players pressed him into service.

But whenever he had a free evening—or often
after some party—he changed locale. A favorite crony
was Capain Donovan of the Joy Street Police Station.
Many a night they prowled together through the narrow
streets of Boston's less attractive neighborhoods. Arthur
Fiedler's insatiable appetite for life in all its manifesta-

tions, helped him to know Boston, as well as hundreds of other cities through such excursions. Men like this Captain found their routine chores lightened by the gay company of the man whose music for the multitudes has given lift to their souls and those of their families.

By now his childhood love of fire engines had matured into another avocation. The clang of the old-fashioned engines rousing Bostonians from their sleep stirred a deep rhythm in the Pops' conductor. Eventually, his own convertible was equipped with a special siren. He wore the helmet of an Honorary Fire Chief, not only in Boston, but ultimately in eighty-five other cities throughout the United States and Canada—even in Japan. Reporters on the fire beat were heard to say, "If he hadn't started fooling around with music, Arthur Fiedler would have been the best fire chief Boston ever had."

Such praise stemmed from the days in the gay 'twenties when he rode the engines with his firehouse pals on special invitation from men who knew that his interest in their calling was as sincere as their own. His explanation of this unusual obsession was given to an interviewer many years later.

"A man must have some avocation, an exciting avocation. . . . My interest has grown. I'm especially intrigued with the science of fire fighting. It takes split second decisions and quick thinking to figure out strategy in fighting big fires. Fire and water are two of the most powerful elements in nature. I love the conflict between the two. It is thrilling to see firemen control the flames. Music is exciting, too."

Thus it was that friends from firehouses and police stations mingled with those from universities and business houses as the green and gold tables in Symphony Hall filled up on the evening of May 7, 1930—all aflame with the excitement of Fiedler's contagious love of music. They rose in feverish ovation as the new permanent conductor stepped onto the podium. It took several minutes before the din of welcoming applause subsided to permit the stirring strains of *Pomp and Circumstance* to respond through that acoustically-perfect auditorium. Arthur Fiedler does not wait for his listeners to quiet. He wins their attention by going ahead. And so on this night—as on all the hundreds which have followed—he swept the crowd into the inaugural of what some of his admirers termed "the Golden Age of the Pops."

The sonorous tones of the March from *Aida* burst full force; but his hand was light and flexible as he led his players through the changeful overture of Mignon. Many a toe tapped beneath the gold-fringed tables as he beckoned the strings into the *Rosenkavalier Waltzes* and wove together the haunting tunes of Romberg's *New Moon*. One reviewer tried to explain the total effect of the evening by declaring that "he always seems to those who really know him like one riding forth in shining armor as did knights of old."

But the Fiedler mission was not to seek the Holy

Grail. It was just to enrich the hearts of the people of Boston with a deeper understanding of the true meaning of *music*—all music that speaks from soul to soul. "My idea," he said, "is nothing but an attempt to blend all types of music. After all, why should a concert consist solely of one type of music? People who go to hear Shakespeare one night may go to a rollicking comedy the next. Those who are fond of fine painting also appreciate a clever caricature."

As he prepared programs for the first season, Fiedler recalled a precept often quoted by his father, "Popular music is familiar music." These words of Theodore Thomas, early conductor of the Chicago Symphony and the New York Philharmonic, became his motto as Fiedler sought to educate the general public to appreciation of the timelessness of classical music, and the snobbish "classical-minded" to understanding of the human appeal of lighter compositions. A Fiedler Pops Program always included "something for everyone"—familiar classical numbers in the first section, semi-classical pieces and a soloist in the middle, topped off, after a second intermission, with excerpts from light operas and occasional arrangements of TV and radio hit commercials. If a piece has merit, he feels that it should be included—be it Vivaldi or Gershwin, Beethoven or Richard Rogers.

Boston audiences were not all ready to accept Fiedler's musical experiments. For three years Casella had sought to "raise the standards of the Pops," insisting that public taste was better than it was commonly given credit

for possessing. Anything as trivial as light opera was considered by him as beneath the dignity of his players!
Skeptics feared that Fiedler's "return to normalcy"
would undo the educational work of his predecessor; and
pessimists insisted that he had no chance of success in
times when lemonade must be served without claret, and
unemployment was reflected in box office receipts.

Fiedler watched audiences sip "Pops punch," and
turned his attention to satisfying musical appetites with
exciting new numbers. This was Tercentennary Year.
Curiosity led him to library stacks, and he added colorful
notes to the Pops programs when he made discoveries like
the fact that America's first symphonic concerts had been
played in an auditorium near Scollay Square under the
direction of Peter Pelham, Sr.

The Music Librarian of the Boston Public Library,
Richard G. Appel, invited the conductor to look over
some rare examples of the first music in America in a
collection stacked away in the gray stone building on
Copley Square. Here he found the original version of
America, composed by William Billings, a Boston-bred
tanner and singing master, first printed in 1770 in the
"New England Psalm Singer or Chorister." Further digging among the old booklets revealed Billings' original
scribbling—written with chalk on a piece of leather. In
faint lettering Fiedler deciphered the words: "Adopted
(sic) to *America* tune . . . arranged for four voices."
Whistling the notes of the first staff, he drubbed on the
table to get the effect of the other three. Appel offered a

piano, and they found that the melody was carried by the alto.

"The tune is interesting," commented the conductor, "but the harmony is very incorrect." And he took it off to his arranger so that his Pops audience might share his discovery.

Novelties of any kind intrigue Fiedler. When he opened his third season in the spring of 1932, he included Mossolov's *Music of Machines*—or *Soviet Iron Foundry*, with a long steel plate suspended from the wall ready for a member of the percussion section to shake at the proper moment. Such a diversion appealed to the conductor as a way to lift the minds from the multiplying worries of prolonged Depression. Actually, program building for that season had been complicated by numerous letters suggesting that he should give musical recognition to the somber mood of the times. He had even consulted a leading psychiatrist before choosing the works to be presented.

"Yes," the professional student of human reactions had concurred with the letter writers, "sad music would be most fitting. Gay music intended to cheer outrages a grieving person as much as if you would introduce frivolous music at a funeral."

But as Fiedler pondered the matter further, he had trusted his own instinct and continued to include the usual variety of marches, waltzes, rhapsodies, and light operas, paired with overtures and symphonies, plus many premiers of works he thought would be entertaining and instructive.

In mid-June he even instituted a "Gay Nineties Night" in complete antithesis to the clamor for gloomy music. Mothballs were shaken out of ancient wardrobes as the audience entered into the spirit of the affair. Discarded vehicles were brought out of storage; but Fiedler's search for a horsecar ended in disappointment when he found that the last one had been disposed of to some enterprising community far away.

His intuition proved correct as the 1932 season became astonishingly successful, with sold-out houses almost nightly. In this, his third year as Pops leader, his two series had become as much a part of Boston as any historic shrine; and the crowds continued to enjoy music for music's sake, regardless of the absence of alcoholic beverages.

In another two years the good-natured audience, gathered for opening night at the Pops, found to their surprise that a special dispensation from the New Deal gave them a choice of wine, in addition to the 3.2 percent beer permitted the year before. Yet only twenty bottles were sold! The audience, accustomed for sixteen years to chocolate, ice cream, and lemonade, were not intrigued. Fiedler gloated as his assumption that people came for music, not for drink, was justified!

Innovations continued to add spice to the programs. Respighi's *Pines of Rome* at the first concert of the 1934 season was augmented by a well-hidden phonograph from which the nightingale trilled in lilting song. *Spanish Night* followed, with much of the audience in costume, and the Hans Wiener Dance Group performing a de Falla ballet, *El Amor Brujo.*

Children's Night, with paper hats and toy watches, did not go over as well with the critics as with the partici- pants. According to the "Christian Science Monitor" . . . "It was amusing and a little pathetic to see members of the Boston Symphony attempting jazz rhythms and to hear them whistle and shout in imitation of the Negroid manner. Apart from the question of suitability, there is the question of capacity. The fact is, if there is one thing the Boston Symphony cannot play, it's jazz."

Nevertheless, the fringe of cherubic faces along both balcony rails and the peals of delight when rosy- winged butterflies fluttered across the stage after the *Wil- liam Tell Overture* said "fie" to such critics. Following the butterflies a procession of small inhabitants of Spain, China, Russia, the Orient; cowboys, George Washington, a wooden soldier, Minnie and Mickey Mouse, Felix, the Cat; Alice, the Mad Hatter; Little Boy Blue; Huck Finn filed in. The conductor distributed prizes according to the amount of applause each received, first prize going to the daughter of a member of the orchestra.

Although the conductor was younger than most of his players—Uncle Benny was still among the violinists— Fiedler's zest for happy living buoyed players and audi- ence throughout the season. His introduction of new music—"first in Boston"—"first in America"—was a challenge to superior performance. In earlier years there had been times when energy seemed to ebb toward the end of the season; but this time the enthusiasm of the closing concert was indistinguishable from that of the opening. Bostonians, like the rest of the world, were probably skimping on necessities; but they wore their old clothes and subsisted on plain food rather than miss the spiritual sustenance offered in Symphony Hall. There had not been a single poor house out of the fifty Pops concerts of that year.

Other unusual experiences highlighted these months. In March Fiedler had conducted his first operetta—de Koven's *Robin Hood* in Jordan Hall—with all the fervor that robust music demands. In July he played the carillon at the Century of Progress Exposition in Chicago—by wire from Symphony Hall. The Esplanade concerts opened in a new shell.

The decision of the Metropolitan District Commissioners to replace the dilapidated temporary wooden shell eased some of Fiedler's worries. Depression had threatened the very existence of his cherished project. Wealthy backers, forced to retrench by continued Depression, were one by one withdrawing support. Public appeals and editorials seeking a wider base of giving in smaller denominations had brought disheartening response. Then, just as even Fiedler optimism began to wane, the announcement that public funds would be used to erect a proper shell brought assurance that official Boston appreciated his contribution to the city's prestige and mental health.

Dr. Barss joined the conductor in long conferences with architects and metal workers as they contributed what came to be known as a "non-electric orchestral amplifier" unique among such structures. The shell was composed of concentric rings of steel. Wooden linings attached to supports left hollow chambers between each of the rings and the steel roof and walls. Each ring was thus built to react to musical vibrations much like the body of a 'cello.

The platform on which the players sat was built in sections, each resembling a table with four-by-four posts for legs. All of them were bolted together and to bars lying across concrete piles. But none of this was permanent. At the end of each season, it would all have to be taken apart and stored in sections, as a protection against winter snow.

All of July and into August thousands of music lovers came nightly to listen to the richer and clearer tones that came from the new shell. The previous year Fiedler had tried out the first full symphony—the *Beethoven Fifth*—at the Esplanade. Now with his better sounding board, he introduced more of the classics which he was determined to make popular through familiarity.

Closing night became a gala. Conductor Fiedler and his orchestra cruised down the Charles. The Maestro, natty in white linen, stepped from the *Flagship Samuel Adams* and mounted the podium. Spotlights played on him as he acknowledged applause after the final encore.

A week later he sailed from Halifax with his cousin, 'cellist Joseph Zimbler, bound for Bermuda and the British West Indies on a well-earned vacation.

CHAPTER FIVE

❦

Musicians Must Eat

ARTHUR FIEDLER'S RELUCTANCE to carry a depressed mood into his Pops concerts did not mean that he was blind to current distress. Rather, as he seemed to pick up the anxiety of those around him, he was able to transmit his own courage and resiliency to those disheartened musicians whose jobs and savings were fast disappearing. He was deeply concerned with the plight of the young and untried, who saw no future in a society straining to keep even the experienced and highly trained employed in any of the arts.

The community recognized his contribution. One evening during an Esplanade intermission, the Medical Director of Suffolk County came to the platform to express appreciation. Dr. McGrath, referring to the current epidemic of suicides, said: "I know of no better remedy for physical and mental fatigue than good music. If many a fellow who had decided to end it all had heard what you have heard and are going to hear tonight, he would have put it off until morning, and maybe forever."

65

Mayor Curley provided constructive official outlet for Fiedler compassion by appointing him chairman of the section on music in an Emergency Committee on Health and Recreation to aid the unemployed. Before this aid was formalized under the National Economic Recovery Act Fiedler had organized three municipal orchestras and four choruses in Boston by 1933.

With the appointment of Harry Ellis Dickson as regular Conductor of the Boston E.R.A. Orchestras, Fiedler found himself co-operating with a congenial younger musician whose professional relationship was to prove helpful through many later years. He had known Dickson as a student who had come to him four years earlier for advice about continuing his musical education in Europe. Fortified with a letter to the Berlin Fiedlers— and three pounds of precious coffee from their son in America—Dickson had won the friendship of Emanuel, Johanna and their daughters. Now, back in a needy America, Dickson welcomed the opportunity to work with Fiedler in common community effort. He frequently handed the baton to the older musician when Fiedler joined him on the Common and thus let the E.R.A. players have the benefit of Fiedler conducting for the second half of a summer program.

Later Dickson became a member of the violin section of the Boston Symphony Orchestra, as well as that of the Pops. In subsequent years, when parts of the Pops programs were broadcast, Fiedler would occasionally use a guest conductor for the second half.

"How come," he said to Dickson one day after a rehearsal, "you haven't asked to conduct? You used to be a conductor! Would you like to take over next week?"

Acceptance of that invitation had far-reaching results, culminating in 1955 when Dickson took Fiedler's place on the podium after the Pops Maestro returned from a strenuous tour to enter the hospital for major surgery. A year later Fiedler appointed his friend as the first, and only, Assistant Conductor for both Pops and Esplanade orchestras.

In the mid-'thirties when these two first worked together, there was a crisis on The Charles. The E.R.A. Chorus requested the privilege of using the new steel shell on Saturday nights—the one "night off" for Esplanade players. In spite of his deep interest in the E.R.A. musical program, Fiedler felt that appearances by extraneous organizations would disturb the continuity of The Esplanade series. He was backed in his stand by the Metropolitan District Commissioners. Indignant citizens wrote "letters to the editor," protesting this discrimination. Editorials took up the charge. Anonymous letters even threatened the life of the man who had until then been so idolized by public music-lovers. One letter, milder in is threats, ended—"Fiedler should at least be dunked in The Charles!"

For a time the quarrel was so serious that Fiedler mounted the podium under police guard. Finally, after the regular series was over, peace was restored. Fiedler offered to direct the E.R.A. civic chorus, usually led by

Dickson, in the Parkman Bandstand on the Common. On August 16th one of the choruses finally appeared in the Shell.

Two years later men familiar with Fiedler talent and musical ability called him into wider service. Walter Piston of the Harvard Department of Music and Dr. Hugo Leichentritt, co-chairmen of the Massachusetts Advisory Committee on American Music, chose Fiedler as guest conductor of the first All-American concert of an augmented E.R.A. Orchestra. Uncounted rehearsal hours welded these ninety musicians into an enthusiastic playing group ready to pack the Boston Opera House for their opening on March 7, 1935. Works by Paine, MacDowell, Hadley, and Schelling were supplemented by unique first performances. Fiedler honored his Boston University faculty colleague, Dr. Carl McKinley, organist of Old South Church, by presenting his *Masquerade;* while the committee's choice of Douglas Moore's *Pageant of P. T. Barnum* as the evening's special feature drew on all of Fiedler's ingenuity with its rich, homey humor and haunting tunes.

Koussevitzky, chatting with reporters during intermission, claimed "this exhibit of American musical art is the most interesting result this emergency has brought up, and a stimulus to all American composers."

The following month Fiedler was among the honored alumni invited to participate in the Tercentennary of the Boston Latin School. Here, on the same platform where the Honorable Joseph P. Kennedy was to be the speaker of the day, the man whose father had once humiliated him by tuning his violin in public lifted his baton to lead a selected group of Boston Symphony players.

It was in a light-hearted mood that Arthur Fiedler shook off his responsibilities once the Pops and Esplanade seasons were over that summer, to depart on his annual trip across the Atlantic. But his gaiety was soon interrupted. His travel companion, with whom he had expected to spend a few care-free weeks in Paris prior to the family visit, died before they landed at Le Havre. Arthur took Dreyfus' body on to Paris, where he put in a phone call to Berlin.

Rosa's voice was agitated as she told him that their mother was critically ill. Arthur left the Dreyfus funeral arrangements to mutual Parisian friends, and caught the night express. As he alighted from the train in the dismal Berlin station, Rosa and her husband greeted him silently.

"Where are the others?" he questioned; but red eyes told him that he was never to hear again the gentle voice that had guided and rewarded him through all his growing years.

After the funeral the group sat in heartbroken conference. Not only was their personal bereavement tragic; their future in Nazi-dominated Germany looked bleak. Elsa, also home from New York, joined her brother in insisting that the others should return to the Land of the Free before Hitler hatred should become

more violent. Rosa and Morris Hochland had already
decided to cast their lot in America. It was harder to
uproot Emanuel and his eldest daughter 'Rika. But before leaving, Elsa and Arthur exacted a promise that the
two would come when proper arrangements could be
made.

Fiedler came home to find a close friend, Henry
Hadley, ill and depressed. While his own mind had been
occupied with family troubles in Germany, Arthur had
been unaware of the struggles Hadley had been through
in attempting to continue and develop his dream of
"Music Under The Stars" in the wooded Berkshire hills.
Only a year before, Fiedler had rejoiced with the composer-conductor over the auspicious first season of the
Berkshire Symphonic Festival, to which Hadley had
brought sixty-five members of the New York Philharmonic to give three August concerts on the Dan R.
Hanna Farm at Interlaken. With benches, stage, and
shell built by W.P.A. labor, the whole plan was geared
to the spirit of the Depression era.

Before he had left for Europe, he had shared in the
general enthusiasm around Boston as plans had been for-
mulating for an enlarged orchestra requested by the Festival Trustees; and a New York press agent was evolving
promotion schemes for bringing many notables to the
opening of the second season. This, Arthur heard, had
been a distinguished occasion. Governors of two states—
Theodore Green of Rhode Island, and Curley of Massachusetts—had shared public welcome with Mrs. James

Roosevelt, mother of the President. Governor Curley had even read dramatic greetings from Max Reinhardt in Austria: "From Salzburg in the Old World" to "Salzburg in the New."

Now the returning traveler learned that in spite of the propitious opening, the season had closed with many problems. Although 9,000 people had crowded the Stockbridge-Lenox area for the musical weekend, the Festival had closed in the red. Car owners complained of the muddy parking lot; musicians, of the lack of imagination in the programs. Critics had written disparagingly of the failure of the Festival in its present form to measure up to the "Salzburg" predictions. Elmore Leffingwell, the press agent, had reported regretfully to the co-ordinating committee that "the music-loving public has reached a point in America where it likes leavened programs or balanced selections . . . these programs should include modern American music, such as Paul Whiteman and Vincent Lopez conduct in their more inspired moments."

Mutual friends in Stockbridge and Pittsfield told Fiedler their worries over Hadley's health—how his physician had stayed by him until the moment he mounted the platform, and how Hadley had primed soloist Rudolph Ganz to be prepared to take over at the final concert should he be unable to complete the evening.

Thus, it was no surprise to Fiedler, after Hadley's resignation was announced in September, to be approached by some members of the Festival Committee

with the idea of bringing the Boston Pops to the Berkshires the following summer. Arthur was elated. Outdoor
concerts were his delight. The Esplanade was proving
that he had his finger on the public music pulse. His
mind was racing with program plans as he took the suggestion to the management of the Boston Symphony
Orchestra.

"Yes," it was agreed. "You could do this well; but
out of courtesy, we should discuss the proposition with
the Maestro. He would not be interested in it himself, of
course, since he always heads for Europe the minute the
winter Symphonies are over!"

Sure of their assumption that Koussevitzky would
not give a second thought to foregoing the cultural opportunities of Paris, Vienna, and London for a struggling
Festival in the horse ring of a Berkshire farm, the two
men knocked on the Maestro's door.

Then, for the first time in his career of mounting
successes, Emanuel Fiedler's "Golden Son" met bitter disappointment. Koussevitzky's prescient mind grasped all
the potentials. He told them how he had dreamed of cre-
ating a Center of Music and Arts in pre-World War days
when he was conducting in Moscow. Now at last the time
had come. *He* would take over this Berkshire Festival
and make Massachusetts' most beautiful natural park a
Center where everyone with intelligent interest and love
for music would find inspiration.

If Arthur Fiedler walked out of that office with
anger and resentment boiling deep, his suave exterior

revealed none of it. In fact, he buried it so completely that just those nearest to him ever knew of the offer. Only when a Fiedler-conducted Pops evening at Tanglewood hit a record attendance for any single concert nearly thirty years later, on a gala August night in 1963 —and the Berkshire Music Center benefitted in the amount of $38,000—could Fiedler speak casually of the opportunity that once might have been his.

Back in that busy season of 1935-1936 Fiedler poured added zest into his task as Chairman of the Music Committee of the Massachusetts Division of W.P.A., and made preparations for the homecoming of his father and sister.

It was a proud moment for father and son when Emanuel celebrated his seventy-seventh birthday by attending the opening of the Pops that spring. His picture with Arthur in the "Boston Traveller" showed him demonstrating how he had played with that same orchestra fifty-one years before. This night in 1936 he pointed to three former pupils, now playing under the conductor they had known as a child. Uncle Benny, Samuel Diamond, and Percy Leveen joined in welcome to the stern instructor, who in the interim had been concert master for the Berlin Opera Comique in addition to his stand among the first violins of the Berlin Philharmonic. He told them that he still practiced two hours a day.

When the Esplanade concerts were resumed Arthur invited his father to show the results of that practice. White-haired Emanuel Fiedler sat erect next to his brother Benny among the first violins that hot July night. Gustave, too, was nearby; while across the podium among the 'cellos he looked at their nephew, Joseph Zimbler. Emanuel's curled and waxed mustache and blue and white polka-dot tie, secured by a carnelian intaglio, emphasized his Old World courtliness. His eyes were on the expressive hands of the grown boy he had first taught to count the beat; but in his mind he seemed to see that older Arthur whose baton he had followed so long ago. The great Nikisch would surely share his pride in the young man who was carrying that name to fame again in a new era of musical adventure.

Intermission came. The other violinists stepped aside to let father follow son off the platform. As the orchestra relaxed in jocular mood behind the Shell, Uncle Benny looked at his older brother.

"Were you nervous?"

"Look!" the old Berliner held out his instrument, "the wood is dry and so are my hands."

Applause for the Brahms C-minor was still echoing. Emanuel turned to trumpeter Joseph Marden, who had joined the Symphony at the same time he had in the distant past.

"Remember when Boston walked out on that?"

As Emanuel observed these changes in American musical taste he began to recognize that his son was having some part in the process. Very soon the younger Fiedler was appointed one of the regular conductors of the new Federal Symphony Orchestra, organized by Nicolai

Sokoloff, who now headed the Federal Music Project of W.P.A. Audiences in New York, Philadelphia, and Washington, as well as Boston, received the impact of Fiedler enthusiasm as he drew applause for Brahms and Wagner, Hindemith and Stravinsky, as well as for familiar waltzes and semi-classical overtures.

Unclocked rehearsals demanded infinite patience while he integrated youngsters unaccustomed to footlights into an orchestra which included veterans like Charles Andrew Vespia, once Victor Herbert's concertmaster. Fiedler was determined to give audiences in the W.P.A. Theatre the best performances a well-trained group of players could produce. A capacity crowd cheered an All-Beethoven concert in New York. He introduced novelties like Ibert's *Divertissement* which had had its world premier in Boston with the Fiedler Sinfonietta. When young Eric Delamater sent him his orchestration of a suite from Rameau's *Dardanus,* Fiedler encouraged the talented composer by a finished presentation.

Not only did he challenge the men who played and the audience who listened, but he was enhancing his reputation as a scholarly as well as a popular conductor. Mingling with other honor guests at a celebration for his former piano teacher, Carl Lamson—then completing twenty-five years of touring with Fritz Kreisler—he could sense musical respect from Bostonians who had heretofore been good-naturedly snobbish about the Pops.

In his heart he began to feel that the time was approaching when his ambition to follow in the footsteps of Nikisch, Muck,and Monteux might be realized. Unexpected expressions of appreciation rewarded the man who had not neglected his regular assignments while carrying the extra load of Federal and State music projects. Two thousand cheering people rose mid-way in a Pops program on July 1, 1938, when a fanfare composed by Walter Piston heralded a surprise. Glittering electric light bulbs suddenly flashed "A—500—F" across the organ pipes of Symphony Hall, signalling the 500th Fiedler-led concert of the Pops—"the longest term ever enjoyed by a conductor of that orchestra."

When The Esplanade opened its tenth season a week later with an All-Wagner program, in honor of the 135th anniversary of the German genius, the largest crowd yet gathered on an opening night sat under the bright moon, refreshed by a fine sailing breeze out of the east. Three announcements made the evening unforgettable. The Board of Trustees of the Boston Symphony Orchestra made public its decision to assume responsibility for the concerts. The Commonwealth of Massachusetts promised an appropriation for their continuance; and the City Fathers told of plans to build a permanent Shell.

This last announcement was, like the concerts themselves, a tribute to Arthur Fiedler's persuasiveness. A fund left to the city by the sister of Edwin M. Hatch to provide "a park, playground, or some other memorial that will accomplish the greatest amount of good for the greatest number of people" had been accumulating in-

terest because no one could agree as to its best use. Once
Fiedler had learned of its existence, he had besieged the
City Hall until he had won the decision to allocate the
money to enhance the pleasure of the unique summer
gatherings that drew all of Boston together under the
stars.

With all of this backing in official circles the conductor now instituted another of his long-dreamed innovations. For ten years he had watched family groups
spreading their blankets on the Esplanade grass each
summer evening to settle down with children of all ages
while his music floated over them. Babies sucked their
bottles and were lulled to sleep as parents shed tensions,
soothed by Mozart and Mendelssohn. Older children
swayed in lithe response to Strauss or Gershwin.

During the 1938 season he decided that these
youngsters deserved concerts of their own. He began
with Saturday mornings, when thousands of children
streamed in from all over Greater Boston. Their eager-
ness made preparations almost more exacting than for
the regular nights. Often he would use guest conductors
for preceding evenings so that he could be alert for the
morning. Any time, he thought, those audiences might
include some future great musician.

As further incentive for the talented, he established a routine of featuring gifted children as soloists.
Little Johnny Frisora, a ten-year-old from Worcester,
played his own composition, *Carnival of Animals* for
ten thousand excited boys and girls. Blind Rosalie Hoff-

man, from the famous Perkins-Watertown School, stirred conductor and audience alike.

Arthur Fiedler's immediate rapport with individual children faded when he faced them en masse. Music was his means of communication; but the youngsters must understand the meaning of what they were hearing. To this end, in his early concerts, he called on his Public Relations Director, Laning Humphrey, to put his ideas into spoken words.

"See if you can recognize the bear," the children were challenged if they were to hear the Finale of the Beethoven Seventh with its famous *Bear Dance*. Or they were asked, "How many of you play the trumpet?" when Ghitalla was to solo in *The Lost Chord*. A performance of this number is traditional at The Esplanade, either for the children, or on some regular night—played to honor Sergeant "Smokey" Walsh of the Metropolitan District Police, who always used to request this number by his Irish compatriot, Arthur Sullivan. The youngsters, however, probably got a bigger thrill out of an encore that was the favorite of the first officer in charge at The Esplanade.

"How do you like the music?" Fiedler would ask Captain Chapman. The reply was always the same, "Fine, if you will play *Turkey in the Straw*."

But it was a childish voice echoing in the Shell— "Oh, I know that piece"— when the strains of von Suppe's *Poet and Peasant Overture* alerted the juvenile audience that really rewarded the conductor. He was determined that America must eventually become the most musical nation in the world; and if that is to happen, the youngest generation must become as accustomed to concerts as to libraries.

Fiedler versatility was well tested that summer of 1938. In addition to the extra time he was giving to children and W.P.A., he was devoting long hours to The Cecilia Chorus preparing for one of the most challenging experiences of his career. Koussevitzky had sought the collaboration of this meticulously-trained organization as he planned the program with which the new Music Shed at Tanglewood would be dedicated.

This new location for the Berkshire Music Festival was the result of a munificent gift to the Boston Symphony Orchestra. Tanglewood with its sweeping lawns, ancient trees, and formal gardens—a place made famous by Nathaniel Hawthorne when he lived in his little red house on the edge of the two-hundred acre Tappan Estate—was offered to Dr. Koussevitzky for this purpose by the sister and daughter of the late banker early in the winter of 1937. During that summer, as in his first one in the Berkshires, Koussevitzky had reluctantly agreed to carry on in a "rain insurance" tent as a substitute for the permanent shelter he had originally stipulated. The imposing Shed now about to be dedicated was there because, on an unforgettable August night in 1937, the gods of Valhalla had offered incontestable competition to a performance of Wagner's *Ride of the Valkyries*. As dark clouds streaked with lightning obscured the moon, and crashing thunder drowned the trumpets while French horns shipped water leaking through the drenched tent, the Maestro had finally laid down his baton. "I cannot compete with the elements!" he declared.

Manager Judd came to the microphone to announce that the concert would go on after intermission, with some changes in the program resulting from storm damage to certain instruments. Then, before the audience could leave, at the close of the evening Founder-President, Miss Gertrude Robinson Smith, climbed onto the stage to announce:

"This storm has proved conclusively the need for a Shed. We *must* raise the necessary $100,000 to build it."

Thirty thousand dollars was pledged before the listeners filed out to pick their way across rain-drenched grass to waiting cars. Even with that encouraging start, not quite enough money had been raised to carry out the elaborate plans drawn by Eliel Saarinen. But a compromise was achieved by which the famous architect allowed Joseph Frantz, an engineer-member of the Committee, to use his blueprints, with modifications to meet the financial resources of the Festival Committee. On the last day of 1937 ground was broken. Workmen struggled on against the hazards of freezes and spring thaws— when trucks were mired in mud. The Shed was completed a month ahead of schedule—on June 4, 1938.

Now on the 4th of August, Arthur Fiedler shared with Koussevitzky in the dedication. Music-lovers from all over the nation applauded expertly trained singers in the Beethoven Ninth and two Bach excerpts.

"Arthur Fiedler deserves no small amount of commendation for the finesse with which he trained the singers," wrote Jay Rosenfeld in the "Berkshire Evening Eagle." "The project of putting chorus and symphony together is no minor matter . . . from the farthermost reaches of the building the combination was perfect . . ."

That summer ended with a trip different from any of his past experiences. As part of the Fiedler effort to encourage American composers he was planning to introduce a symphony by William Grant Still, an eminent Negro musician, for a *Pops Afro-American Night* in his 1939 Boston season. Those stimulating evenings in the Negro cafés of Norfolk, Virginia, had left a lasting impression. He had always wanted to give recognition to the folklore of the black race. Now he needed a voodoo drum to give authenticity to the coming performance. He turned to Puerto Rican-born Sanromá for advice. Why not, suggested his long-time friend, make a trip to Haiti, with a stop-over at San Juan, where Sanromá was expecting to visit relatives soon?

The idea appealed to the adventurous conductor. Now that all his family were in Ameria, it was time to learn about places other than Europe. His friend, Philip Clark, President of the New England Confectionery Company, and a music-lover by avocation, accepted his invitation to go along.

The start of that journey was typical of Fiedler

pace. There were cocktails in Stockbridge before a Boston Symphony at Tanglewood. Supper followed the concert, in the Springfield home of the Hollis Carlisles. Little was left of the night by the time he reached Boston; but he breakfasted at the Copley-Plaza before giving his o.k. to fifty new Pops recordings. Then the Musical Director of RCA Victor, Charles O'Connell—who recounts this whirlwind finish to a Fiedler season in his book, "The Other Side of the Record"—drove him to the Clarks' home in Lexington. Mrs. Clark tried out a new recipe for the farewell party. Fresh peaches spiked with brandy were in each champagne glass as many friends drank to the success of the coming adventure. Then the three men started for New York, taking turns sleeping in the back seat of the Zephyr while one drove. At the dock, they found the Hochlands ready to wave them off on an old Puerto Rican banana boat, the *San Jacinto*.

As the ship came alongside the San Juan dock, Clark looked down on the cheering crowd. "Your fame has preceeded you," he said jestingly to his companion. But they soon discovered that the excited Puerto Ricans were welcoming student heroes of the Spanish Civil War, young men who had risked their lives against the Communists in the recent Revolution.

Sanromá was the sole person interested in the Boston visitors; but his hospitality extended through a gay week. Then Fiedler and Clark flew off to Trujillo City, enroute to Haiti. Here they had a problem. No one could leave the Dominican Republic without a police permit and they had arrived on a three-day holiday— Saturday, Sunday, and Monday, when the dedication of the new airport would give excuse for an extra day of leisure. The pair sat dejectedly in the lobby of the Colon Hotel.

At a nearby table a dapper dandy was drinking beer. Learning from the desk clerk that he was the Colonel of Police, the Bostonians offered to buy drinks for all three. But the man was haughty, insisting that the office was closed and he could do nothing about their predicament. Clark produced a letter from the Dominican Consul in Boston, asking special consideration for a "large user of much sugar and chocolate." His companion was merely mentioned as a "musician."

"What do you play?" asked the Colonel, turning to Fiedler.

With his most winning smile, the Pops conductor remarked, "Once I played the tuba!"

Sullen eyes changed expression. "Oh," said the police chief, "I played the tuba in Tuskegee." He accepted their proferred drink and as they spoke in the musical jargon that knows no international boundaries, he confessed that his original rudeness was a hangover from resentment of the "Jim Crow" treatment he had received in Florida. He admitted that these two were different, and they left the table with the signature of the Colonel of Police written with great flourish on their permission to leave. "Many people can't read," he admonished as his pen made the ornate last letter, "but always show them your credentials."

When they reached Port-au-Prince in Haiti, Clark was satisfied that the reputation of his friend had indeed gone ahead. A small record shop displayed a Fiedler recording in its window, the jacket picturing the colorful man who walked beside him. Boys loitering by the shop door recognized him, too, and word went out along the narrow streets. Arthur was kept busy inside the shop for some time autographing the surprising number of recordings produced by the excited proprietor. Then an imposing man walked in, and the shop owner introduced Sylvio Cato, the only Haitian ever to win an Olympic award—"in the broad jump," he told them.

"Come on over to my bar," Cato urged as he acknowledged the introduction.

Over rum punch Fiedler explained their reasons for coming to Haiti.

"Well, we'll see what Dante Bellegard can do about it," Cato said as he took down the wall telephone to call the diplomat who, he told them, had once held Haiti's most important foreign post—Ambassador to France.

Bellegard hastened to meet the visitors who had shown such interest in native music. Quickly he arranged a trip to a camp where they could hear the wanted voodoo drums. Fiedler, tanned from his days on the Puerto Rican beaches, mingled, unnoticed, in the crowd, who accepted him as some Haitian aristocrat, probably one with noble French blood. Presently a band brought in the drums, which Cato, who had come with them, identified as of three types—bass, baritone and tenor. Arthur stooped to examine them without observing that they had been sprinkled with dust in some mysterious rite. One of the Haitians saw the stranger's hand on the drum, and all hell broke loose!

"Run for your lives," shouted Cato, and the Boston visitors dashed down the road, where their trusted driver was waiting, jumped in and sped for the city.

After a few days' cooling off period they found their way to another camp in the hills, quite a distance from Port-au-Prince. Light from a full moon filtered through the tropical foliage. Like a modern jazz group, where each dancer tried impromptu variations in his individual step, the strange rhythm accelerated under the spell of his weird light. Fiedler and Clark joined in, dancing alone among the natives, highly charged by rum served in used tin cans. The stuff felt like one-hundred proof as it burned down their throats, but they were rewarded for their camaraderie with the purchase of the wanted drums.

Fiedler had to fly back to fulfill an engagement in Boston, leaving his treasures to be hand-carried by Clark on the boat. The drums created a sensation when a red cap took them from a taxi at Grand Central Station. He gave a professional thump on one of them. As this resounded in the Grand Concourse, Clark was followed by a procession of grinning porters when he descended the stairs to cross the crowded waiting room enroute to his Boston train.

Not many of Fiedler's "Special Pops Nights" required such extensive preparations; but he is always alert to an opportunity to attract audiences. When Crown Prince Olav arrived from Norway with the Crown Princess Martha, the spring-decorated Symphony Hall echoed with haunting Grieg music, recalling the grassy slopes of Troldhaugen for the Norwegian-American audience who knew the great composer's home facing an arm of the Hardanger Fjord.

During all these busy months Fiedler's usefulness to the Federal Music Project was increasing. His knowledge of the music of early America made him invaluable to the groups planning the second All-America Music Festival. Some of the music from Colonial and Revolutionary times which he had unearthed in old shops and libraries in Boston was woven into the repertoire of concerts all over the United States. Thousands of musicians participated in the three-day historical event that colored music appreciation classes and concerts with patriotism.

When the official report of the Federal Music Project was released in the autumn of 1939, Fiedler was listed along with Stokowski, Ormandy and other nationally prominent conductors as "contributing greatly to the tremendously expanded musical consciousness discernible in the past three years." As national support was gradually replaced by state and local underwriting, he continued in his guidance of young musicians as

Director of the Youth Administration Music Project in Massachusetts with the added responsibility of becoming Musical Consultant to the United States Veterans Administration in Boston. Fiedler preparations for summer music brought enthusiastic comment from the "Boston Transcript" which said:

"The Boston Common has heard a great deal of music from the time when British drums and fifes sounded in the long ago; but it probably never had so full a season as that to be given by W.P.A. musicians this summer."

CHAPTER SIX

"Foster Father" to Talented Youth

"KIDS DON'T BRUSH their teeth unless you make them."

A group of Boston mothers gathered for an A.A.U.W. meeting in the large auditorium of Filene's department store exchanged knowing nods as these unexpected words came from the Pops conductor. But his next sentence told them that he was not straying from his subject, "The Influence of Music in the Home."

"It's the same with music," he continued. "You have to make them practice. My father did, and I'm glad he did. . . . Musical training helps their arithmetic, teaches rhythm, improves memory and coordination and gives them an interest in something great."

Having no one of his own to whom he could pass on the precepts that he had learned from Emanuel, the bachelor conductor never missed an opportunity like

89

this. Today's speech was on the air, and he broadcast an urgent plea to parents everywhere to expose their off-spring to the best on records and radio. He told them that just as libraries open young minds to the world's storehouse of knowledge, so these new media bring musical language to all who will listen. He painted vivid sketches of great composers who had been reared in the atmosphere of fine music and impressed on these mothers their obligation to detect talent and foster it.

He practiced what he preached daily, offering the platforms of Pops and Esplanade as debut stages for potential artists. Six-year-old Goldie Luipold fascinated him; and he called Emanuel in to listen to the child's audition.

"I never heard anything like it," the conductor said to his father "The girl has absolute pitch. She is able to identify every note. What's more, she possesses spontaneous genius along with the poise and personality necessary for a successful performance."

Goldie, like hundreds of others, could perform at her best for Fiedler because he is always so natural with children that they forget everything except mutual en-joyment of what they are doing. They could not be self-conscious in the presence of a man as out-giving as this one, listening with the expectancy of a prospector search-ing for gold.

When little Charles Castleman stood on a granite block at the entrance to the Esplanade Shell to play his child-size violin, Fiedler knew he had found real talent.

He tried out the five-year-old's musical knowledge by whistling tune after tune. The answer was correct every time. Years later when Fiedler watched young Castleman receive his degree in Music from Harvard University, memories of the boy's debut at a Children's Esplanade and his many performances at both the Shell and the Pops flooded to mind.

Fiedler's associates shared their own discoveries with him, never hesitating to ask him to listen to their children or pupils. Thus the "family" tradition of the Boston Symphony grew like the Fiedler father-son-uncle-cousin group. 'Teen-age Roger Voisin, son of a Boston Symphony trumpeter, began by playing the signal call for Esplanade players to re-assemble after intermission. Soon the audiences began to hear that clear sound in duets with his famous father, and eventually Roger sat in the Principal's chair of the trumpet section in the Boston Pops Orchestra. The first percussionist brought his thirteen-year-old daughter to audition. Not long afterward Joanne Smith was bowing to an Esplanade audience as they applauded her performance of the opening movement of a Mozart piano concerto.

Librarian Leslie Rogers burst into the office he shared with Fiedler, ecstatic over the rare tone of Manuel Valerio's clarinet after a Conservatory recital. "Let me hear him," the conductor suggested; and the young man who later became Principal clarinetist of the Pops was soon listed as a guest soloist.

Almost any time players begin to tune up for a

concert under Fiedler, he can look around and point out
someone who made a debut with him. There is pianist
Leo Litwin, an early pupil of Sanromá, who appeared
first at the Pops, playing the difficult *Rhapsody in Blue*
after Fiedler's close friend asked him to listen to the
promising youth. Through all the years since then, Litwin—who now as a sideline edits a magazine on Covered
Bridges—has been a Fiedler standby. He even married
the Maestro's secretary! Not only could Litwin substitute for Sanromá if necessary, but he is always ready
with his own solos and with pupils—like blind Rosalie
Hoffman, who was awarded a scholarship to study under
him by the Boston Aid to the Blind, or Stephen Steinberg, winner of the National Orchestral Society's award
as the outstanding junior high school musician.

Sheldon Rotenburg, in the violin section, was discovered by Fiedler when Stokowski asked him to hold
try-outs for the All-American Youth Orchestra. Only
twenty of the applicants for the proposed Good Will
Tour of South America were selected to play for Stokowski; but as Fiedler listened to aspiring performers on
every instrument from strings to percussion—except
piano, saxophone and mandolin, which were barred—he
found a nucleus for his own N.Y.A. Orchestra in men
like young Rotenburg. These young people—by stipula-
tion under twenty-five—came from all over Massachusetts; and Fiedler found his musical foster family enlarged with new talent ready to perform on his own
regular programs.

Guest soloists chosen from the Esplanade that summer of 1940 walked onto a fabulous new stage, as the summer series opened with the dedication of the Hatch Shell. Even planes soaring to and from Logan Airport were ordered to change course to insure quiet as thirty-one thousand people gathered on the banks of The Charles. Emanuel and 'Rika sat in comfortable chairs beyond ropes separating special guests from the crowd.

In front of them the luminous surface of the cocoa-brown Burma teak lining of the new concrete Shell reflected burnished trumpets and glowing cymbals. And the beauty of its granite facing—grey-green to match surrounding shrubbery at the lower level and the pink of New Hampshire mountains above—drew their eyes to study the names of great composers chiseled into the hard surface. They thought of the hours of study Arthur had devoted to that selection as he and Koussevitzky had culled out fifty names from the ninety-seven orginal choices. Only two men then living—Richard Strauss and Jan Sibelius—had been included among those considered worthy of this permanent remembrance.

As Arthur signaled his players to begin, rich resonance filled the evening air. His family agreed that Dr. Barss had been right in specifying the use of this durable jungle wood as the perfect sounding board for outdoor acoustics.

During the months of construction Emanuel had often joined his son in watching workmen incorporate the many facilities the conductor had envisioned for the comfort of his orchestra. Tuning rooms, showers, and lockers all had modern equipment; but it was the rehearsal room planned by Arthur for his special needs that brought them the greatest satisfaction.

It was here that Eleanor Roosevelt came in 1941 to listen to the rehearsal for the first public concert of the N.Y.A. Orchestra—later given in Jordan Hall. A few months later Sir Thomas Beecham sat in this same room watching young players whose undivided attention justified his praise. "You can be very proud of your orchestra," the British conductor remarked to Fiedler as they left the Shell.

That same spring offered opportunity to participate in another civic project designed to encourage young talent. When the Boston Symphony Orchestra joined with the "Boston Herald" and the RCA-Victor Company in a venture called the *Musiquiz,* the Pops conductor was invited to direct the Pension Fund Benefit concert which inaugurated the contest. This setting was quite different from his well-equipped new Shell or the splendid Symphony Hall. Here he stepped onto a slightly-raised disc-shaped stage in the center of the prize ring of the Boston Garden, encircled by the musicians. Around them sat ten-thousand people who had paid twenty-five cents a seat. "It took a little double and triple thinking," he explained, "but it was not really too difficult to conduct."

After two elimination rounds in which judges rated the hundreds of papers identifying numbers played first by the orchestra and, in the second try-out, on records, along with short essays about the composers, Fiedler came to Symphony Hall one hot summer morning to greet fifty-four semi-finalists. With characteristic courtesy he softened the strain of competition by suggesting that everyone be served cooling "Pops punch" before they settled down to the task. His own duty as one of the judges was time-consuming but rewarding as the papers revealed much progress toward his goal of a musically literate America.

Finalists were announced at The Esplanade, the first award being divided between two men after the discovery that one of them had the advantage of employment in a record shop. Then the announcer said: "The second prize goes to a young man from Sharon, Connecticut, Leonard Bernstein, a graduate of Harvard University. The prize was to have been a deluxe trip to the Berkshire Festival; but the recipient already has a scholarship to study at Tanglewood under Maestro Koussevitzky. Thus the committee has decided to convert the prize into its money value of $150. But, as Mr. Bernstein wrote in his paper that he hopes to become a conductor, Mr. Fiedler now asks him to come to the podium to conduct the Prelude to *Die Meistersinger* as a final and extra prize."

The slender youth, who in a few more years would rank among the great musicians of his era, sprang to the stage, his dark eyes radiant in response to the welcoming smile of the man who had arranged this unexpected conducting debut. As Arthur Fiedler shook the hand of this younger alumnus of the Boston Latin School, recognition of rare talent tightened his grip. Here was an aspiring artist with both intelligence and spiritual fire. Whatever opportunities Fiedler might offer toward developing these obvious gifts would be placed at Bernstein's command.

Fiedler was aware of the young prize-winner's brilliance as a pianist. He invited him to appear as soloist with the eighty-piece N.Y.A. Orchestra scheduled to appear in New Bedford in October. Bernstein accepted. As the concert neared, a reporter from the ship-building city came up to Boston to interview Fiedler during a rehearsal in the Esplanade Recreation Building. At the half-time break, co-conductor Alexander Thiede stepped up, ready to take the baton; but Fiedler would not leave. Oblivious of time or expenditure of energy, he stayed with the men to assure the best possible rendition of Ravel's piano concerto with Bernstein at the piano. Over and over he rehearsed the vicious attack from the brasses, which he deemed so important to the total effect.

"Why do you do all this?" the visitor inquired.

"Because I love it!" Fiedler's reply glowed with satisfaction.

Then, in a rare moment of relaxation, he continued, "When I auditioned the youth orchestra under Stokowski, I found so many promising players in New England that I wanted to keep a Massachusetts group together. I am training these young people for musical careers. Some have been placed in Houston, some in Indiana, some even in jazz bands. We started in December, 1940, in the Shell rehearsal room. Soon we outgrew it and had to come over to this building."

On the night of the New Bedford concert, there was an unusual revelation of the practical side of Arthur Fiedler. In the middle of the Ravel, "the extremely able young pianist" was stymied when a key refused to function. The conductor held up his palm to indicate a pause, stepped down from the podium, loosened the key and drew all the performers back onto the difficult beat as if this were the order of the day.

Three years after the Musiquiz, Koussevitzky precipitated a situation which might have disheartened a lesser man than the Pops Maestro. For the first time in his thirty years with the organization, Fiedler's name was listed as a guest conductor for a regular pair of Boston Symphony winter concerts. Announcements for the season listed Arthur Fiedler, not only with such veterans as Mitropolous and George Szell, but also with Koussevitzky's protegé, Leonard Bernstein, so recently presented in the Esplanade debut. As fate—or the Russian Maestro —decreed, it happened that Bernstein's contract was honored that year, while Fiedler waited ten more years for recognition of his own serious musical standing in the city of his birth. Just before the pair of concerts scheduled as Fiedler's, word came that the Brazilian composer-conductor Heitor Villa-Lobos would be available for that one date only. Koussevitzky presented his dilemma to the Pops conductor. Fiedler bowed out gracefully; and a disappointed critic recorded that the concerts "probably emphasized the good neighbor policy, but musically it got us nothing."

Not even the man who wrote those kind and revealing words would be allowed to know the depths of that disappointment to Arthur Fiedler. But whatever shadow then momentarily darkened his bright path, it disappeared like an eclipse of the sun. Undoubtedly he could understand the disillusionment of others better for that unhappy trick of fortune; he drew even closer to his men and his responsive public as he went on his way with the pride of a foster parent in the success of aspiring youth.

The many artists whose rewards for practice and study brought them to perform at Pops or Esplanade did not often attain the prominence of a Leonard Bernstein. But they received encouragement for what they brought, and good-natured criticism if that was what they needed. Sometimes an inexperienced soloist comes to rehearsal unequipped to play with a major orchestra. His technique and interpretation may have been of high quality when he was auditioned; but the task of integrating his own rhythms into the pace of eighty or more men and women who know so well the significance of every motion of Fiedler's hands and body may well prove unnerving. The Maestro stops them all. Then with infinite patience and descriptive direction he leans over the piano, score in hand, pulling the young person into the group with the force of a magnet.

Those who can trace the beginnings of their careers

to this steadying influence are legion; and their names
are as kaleidoscopic as the races that have sought freedom
in America. Luise Vosgerchian, daughter of an Armenian grocer, at twenty, was the youngest piano soloist in
The Esplanade's sixteen years when she performed in
August of 1944. As she climbed the stone steps she
tripped over a floor-length gown of moire taffeta.

"That's a sign of luck," whispered Arthur Fiedler
as he grabbed her arm with nonchalant courtesy, adding,
fiercely, "now bow!"

She played the Grieg piano concerto flawlessly—
without a full orchestra rehearsal. Thundering applause
rang from twenty-five thousand clapping hands, but what
she would never forget, was Arthur Fiedler's spontaneous
"Well done, my girl!"

A few years later it was the tiny (not quite five feet)
daughter of the pastor of the Norwegian Lutheran
Church in Cambridge who played that same concerto.
Alice Lillegard, then only seventeen, looked demure in a
homemade white dress, but her strong fingers were alive
with devotion to her country's musical idol.

The former conductor of the Persian Symphony
who had come from Teheran to join the Portland, Maine,
Symphony and later to become a faculty member at the
Boston Conservatory, brought his young son along when
he was guest conductor for the Pops. Leon Gregorian,
who had started piano studies in Teheran at the age of
five, appealed to Fiedler. Several times The Esplanade
audiences delighted in his playing.

From France, from Russia, from Holland came

well-trained young soloists to make debuts under Fiedler, but perhaps none was more beloved than Tung Kwong-kwong from Shanghai. As her delicate fingers flew over the keys the little Chinese student brought credit to her musical parents and to her teachers—Mario Paci, a pupil of Listz, in Shanghai, and at the New England Conservatory where she was a second-generation student. More than once Fiedler included her on both Pops and Esplanade programs, never losing touch after she met and married violinist Ma Si Hon, also among his favorite guest soloists.

Special Nights at the Pops likewise brought opportunities to talented young people of various races and backgrounds. When the hard-won voodoo drum added reality to Afro-American Night, Fiedler had presented the first Negro guest artist, Mrs. Doris Dandridge Harris —forerunner of numerous others who had their "firsts" on this platform. Among them Charles McCabe, later concert-master of the Philadelphia Philharmonic, was the first Negro violinist to make a recording with the Pops. A. Jack Thomas of Baltimore came as the first Negro guest conductor; and child prodigy pianist, Philippa Schuyler of New York, performed on one of the later Colored-American Nights.

Fiedler's large family of musical foster children includes composers as well as performers. Perhaps his keen interest in these young people stems from his early association with George Gershwin, who once shared his Boston apartment. Admiration for Gershwin's capacity for hard work and his memories of listening to night-long harmonizing on the apartment piano have made Fiedler one of the most understanding interpreters of his friend's works. When *Rhapsody in Blue* was written, it was hard to find an artist willing to perform it, but Sanromá was eager to play the new number. The Fiedler recording, with his Puerto Rican associate at the piano, is one of the early Gershwin platters. As part of a gala Pension Fund concert at the Pops, Fiedler presented Gershwin's *Second Rhapsody*—originally called *Rhapsody in Rivets,* which the composer had described in a letter from California as "an attempt to write a serious piece in spite of the weather." When Fiedler took this number with him on his first tour of South America it made such a hit that he was invited to return the next season to Buenos Aires to give an all-Gershwin Concert.

Fiedler recordings of excerpts from *Porgy and Bess* and other Gershwin adaptations of the American idiom, as well as his recordings of Bernstein's *Fancy Free* and *West Side Story* soon ranked among "best sellers."

Arthur Fiedler does not expect a composer to rank with a Gershwin or a Bernstein to be included on his programs. Any music, correct and with appeal, would be introduced. Just as he sought out unusual early Americana or used his Sinfonietta to acquaint Boston with some half-forgotten bit of Old World music, so he used the Pops and The Esplanade to present local composers whom he considered worthy.

There was Alan Hovhaness, an Armenian whose

music was more appreciated in London than in Boston. Koussevitzky would not deign to notice it, but Fiedler successfully brought out one of his smaller tone poems at the Pops.

A young waiter, Anthony Rosato, dedicated a haunting melody to his mother and slipped it into the mail to Fiedler. *Rosina* became so popular that it was repeated at The Esplanade three times—the last as a memorial to the proud immigrant woman who had so happily encouraged her talented son.

During Fiedler's years with the Federal Music Project and his advisory position with the Veterans' Administration, he was always ready to listen with an understanding, as well as critical ear. Once convinced the composition has merit, there is no limit to his effort to perfect and present it.

Thus it was that when a Gray Lady at the Cushing Veterans' Hospital in Framingham, Massachusetts, told him about her attempt to improve the morale of a paralyzed sailor Fiedler paid a personal call on that young man, Robert Grant, Jr. He found Grant to be a victim of multiple sclerosis, with only one still-mobile finger. With that Grant demonstrated what he had achieved after Mrs. Davidson, the Gray Lady, had wheeled him in to the piano in the hospital recreation room. He told Fiedler that he had always loved music, but had never thought of composing until Mrs. Davidson suggested that he try to work out a melody for his poem, *Evening Prayer,* which he had shown to her. With his one good finger he had been able to share with her in notes what had been humming in his mind.

Arthur Fiedler promised to come back. This time he brought the official arranger from the Pops. A few weeks later twenty-five thousand people cheered the composer as Grant sat in his wheel chair at The Esplanade on a warm summer night. Fully orchestrated, *Evening Prayer* brought such applause that the number was repeated. The father of the former Navy boxer and Dartmouth graduate told Fiedler that the lad's invalid mother could not attend. Quickly the Maestro ordered a recording to be made for her.

One of the first arrangers on the Fiedler-led Pops staff was discovered on a Harvard Night. Undergraduate Leroy Anderson was invited to guest-conduct one of his own arrangements. This was so good that Fiedler proposed that he do some more, thus leading to some of the most popular novelties now associated with the Pops all over the world—such as *Fiddle Faddle,* dedicated to Arthur Fiedler.

Anderson's *Syncopated Clock* had its first performance on a Military Night when the composer returned to Boston from World War II service in Iceland. Now it makes a perfect encore for the Haydn *Clock Symphony* when children on The Esplanade have "listened to the ticking" and clapped for more.

Even Fiedler, the "Fire Buff," can find his avocation linked to his profession. One afternoon he and Anderson were chatting casually in the Symphony Hall

Green Room. Ted Mossman, composer of the popular air, *'Til the End of Time,* joined them just as the Maestro said of a new tune Anderson was playing over for him,

"That should have words. With words, your 'Serenata' would be a gold-plated hit on the popular market. It has a Latin zoom that would suit Sinatra's voice—or Bing's."

"A natural," chimed in Mossman, "but it needs a sharp lyric. I'd like to write if I could find a jumping off place."

A siren screeched past on Massachusetts Avenue. "Fire Chief" Fiedler jumped from his chair, pulling on his coat as he dashed out the back stairs. His own convertible stood at the curb as always, identified by his honorary "FDB" plate. With his own shrill blast he followed "hook and ladder No. 15" out of sight of his friends.

Three quarters of an hour later Fiedler puffed back into the Green Room, to find the two composers still trying out ideas on the grand piano.

"You should have seen it," he exclaimed, as he shook the cinders out of his hair and looked down at his smudged trousers. "What a fire! The whole place was aflame!"

"That's it—the jumping off place!" Mossman sniffed the smoke. . . . "Aflame . . . everything's aflame . . . no, my heart's aflame . . . gimme a pencil."

Quickly the scribe grabbed an old program, turned it over and wrote a lyric based on the phrase "my heart's aflame." New York's Tin Pan Alley soon picked up the swinging ditty which this trio of noted musicians had whipped out with the unsuspecting aid of Boston's Fire Department!

From Tin Pan Alley to a recognized musical publication was a natural step for peripatetic Arthur Fiedler. His philosophy of help to young orchestras found expression in an article on that subject in "Etude" for November, 1949, as told to Rose Heylburt.

"Youngsters are exposed to good music in school orchestras exactly as school games inculcate a taste for sports," he wrote, adding that to conduct such a group is "in some respects harder than to conduct the Boston Symphony." In this article he insisted that players should always be grouped so that every one of them can see the conductor out of the corner of his eye; and that strings, reeds, brass, and percussion must learn to "speak" precisely with the conductor's beat, not a flash late. He urged, too, that young players should realize at the beginning that accurate reading of music is as important as practicing scales; and that they should familiarize themselves with works they were most likely to play by listening to good records.

Thus, these foster children—the coming generation of American musicians, whether personal proteges, readers, or listeners—benefitted by Arthur Fiedler's endless investment of time as he used every medium at his command to encourage young people in their understanding of music as an essential part of life.

CHAPTER SEVEN

❦

A Family of His Own

"I CARRY ONLY ONE baby picture," Arthur Fiedler is wont to say to intimates. "I waited for Ellen to grow up," he explains as he draws from his wallet a charming likeness of the little girl who used to play in another room with Lydia Fuller while he rehearsed with the Governor's wife.

The Fuller home was across the street from a large brick house on Beacon Street belonging to Dr. Bottomley, a famous Boston surgeon. The two families were so close that Ellen Bottomley, her three brothers and younger sister always called the lovely soprano "Aunt Ollie," and it was Ellen who replied to Governor Alvan Fuller's question—"And who am I?"—"why, of course. you're 'Uncle Allie.'"

It had been a sad morning when Mrs. Fuller met her young accompanist at the door, saying with choking voice, "I cannot rehearse today. There has been a great tragedy across the street. Dr. Bottomley dropped dead from a heart attack this morning!"

Later, when the daily song practice was resumed, the Governor's wife had asked Arthur, "Would you mind if Mrs. Bottomley comes in while we go over the songs? She loves music; but she does not feel equal yet to going out to concerts."

Young Fiedler soon became accustomed to seeing this neighbor, dressed in deep mourning, sitting quietly at the far side of the big drawing room.

It was not here, however, that Mrs. Bottomley's daughter first felt the impact of Arthur Fiedler. Ellen was about seven when "Aunt Ollie" came to sing at an Assembly at Sacred Heart Convent. The little girl was seated in the front row, her large eyes riveted, not on the singer, but on the handsome young man at the piano.

The guest artists were invited to stay for lunch. As the Reverend Mother came to escort the group, she caught sight of the child.

"Why, here is Ellen!" the warmth of tone revealed her fondness. "Did you like the concert, dear?"

Then, turning to the accompanist,

"Of course, you know Arthur Fiedler?"

Ellen dropped her eyes and curtsied.

"Yes, I—I think so," she murmured.

The casual handshake that followed had significance far beyond what either of them could have dreamed. But that day they had gone their separate ways, outwardly oblivious to each other.

Arthur, then the youngest member of the Boston Symphony, became accustomed to surging crowds of

'teen-age autograph seekers at the back entrance to Symphony Hall. Many a time Serge Koussevitzky passed
through this group unheeded while eager hands held
their programs out to the popular bachelor-violist.

This *bon vivant* story teller *par excellence* became
a welcome guest at dinner tables. Summer adventures
incident to those annual family visits in Berlin furnished
material for intriguing tales. Lively accounts of camel
driving in North Africa, where he and Symphony harpist Cella had gone in search of native music after a sojourn in Germany, enlivened Boston circles in the following winter. A good laugh always followed the story of
their trip to the Berlin barber in preparation for this adventure. They had warned the family of their intention
to have heads shaved clean; but dinner time had found
Arthur's shining dark hair intact. His equally handsome
friend looked like an escaped prisoner.

"After I saw Cella, I changed my mind," Fiedler
always admits.

Another summer he and a cousin took a second
walking trip from Berlin to the Black Forest, with many
a stop along the way to raise their steins in toasts to
pretty fräuleins. He may not have confessed that part to
his Boston hostesses, but his masculine friends relish the
way he gave his telephone number—"Beacon 0999—all
the girls in Berlin used to say it!"

During these years while little Ellen was growing
up, Arthur Fiedler found safety for his bachelor status
in numbers. As one columnist noted, "If he is wearing a

blue shirt, a blue double-breasted suit, blue socks—and is engrossed in a *tête-à-tête* with any one of a hundred girls—it's Arthur Fiedler relaxing."

The miniature brass fiddler which served as a knocker on his Commonwealth Avenue apartment door was lifted by gay companions, who gleefully accepted his description of himself as "happily unmarried," and revelled in the good cooking of housekeeper Louise Smith.

All this was Arthur Fiedler on the surface. The man the world did not know was the devoted son, sending his money across the sea to ease the difficult days of the Berlin family; saving enough to bring father and sister to America after the mother's death. That Arthur had not forgotten the appealing child at the Convent who had curtsied and fleetingly held his hand. He heard about her now and then from "Aunt Ollie," who described her graduation from Sacred Heart and told him that she had gone to L'Ecole Vinet in Lausanne. Then she had spent another year traveling in Switzerland and France.

They finally met as adults when he was directing a symphonic pageant for the benefit of disabled World War I veterans in Boston in 1932. One of the Fuller family's many charitable concerns, the Christopher Shop, sponsored this show. Among the acts a dance group led by Lydia Fuller brought to life the famous Zuloaga painting, *Gypsy Dance,* which hung on the wall of the Governor's house. Eighteen-year-old Ellen Bottomley was one of the dancers, fascinated by Sanromá's guitar playing.

Her partner nudged her. "Mr. Fiedler is pointing at *you*, Ellen."

"Wave your fan in time!" bristled the conductor. The staccato command struck deep.

"Is he married?" Ellen whispered to "Aunt Ollie" when the rehearsal was over.

Arthur Fiedler married! The absurdity of the question brought tears of laughter to Viola Fuller's eyes. That smart bachelor prided himself on his freedom. The sterling used in his Commonwealth Avenue menage was marked "a"-"f" across a bar of music. He even resented the maternal solicitude of his housekeeper who understood so well his erratic hours and his pampered taste buds.

Ellen did not see it as a joke. The magnet hold of that penetrating personality had grasped her heart. The next time their eyes met was in the Fuller home. "Aunt Ollie" was presenting a protegé, Ruth Posselt, in a debut concert. Ellen, now one of the season's debutantes, was passing out programs at the head of the steep stairs leading up from the lower hall to the spacious music room above. Her pale pink crepe, swathed in beads of deeper hue around the hips, set her off in vibrant contrast to Lydia Fuller's black velvet. She stood there, gracious and blooming, as Maestro Koussevitzky came in with the debonair Pops conductor. The young violinist and Sanromá were playing the Caesar Franck sonata, and the three stood close until the number was finished. Then Ellen seated the celebrities where she could watch their faces as the program continued.

When other guests had left, "Aunt Ollie" suggested that she act as special hostess for Arthur Fiedler as they took the Maestros in to supper. Her hand shook so that she could scarcely hold her coffee cup as she sat for the first time beside the man whose life would eventually be interwoven with hers.

But a decade elapsed before that pair, later so completely identified together by the Fiedler-loving public, could overcome all the obstacles that threatened their happiness. Age, religion, family background all stood between them. Yet as the years slipped by, Arthur's place in the Fuller-Bottomley circle became more intimate. Ellen's three brothers liked him. He was an accepted part of every celebration when the group gathered at the Governor's summer home facing the white-capped Atlantic at Rye Beach, New Hampshire. But Mother Bottomley refused to take seriously her daughter's attachment to Boston's "number one ladies' man"!

Ellen's Junior League associates also regarded Arthur Fiedler as merely a "family friend" until they needed a director for their newly-formed Glee Club. Ellen sang with them. To their amazement the Maestro of the Pops took on this new assignment with alacrity. Post-rehearsal dates were easy to make, especially if one

In the spring of 1930 Arthur Fiedler became the 18th conductor of the Boston Pops and its first Boston-born conductor.

PHOTO BY JOHN B. SANROMA

"Bostonians ought to get a kick out of the 'Bostonia,'"
Arthur Fiedler remarks, as Keith Brown, the composer
(right) and Jacobus Langendoen, orchestrator (left) register
their pleasure in his verdict.

Arthur Fiedler studies a scor
for a Pops concert in the earl
'thirties.

Ellen Bottomley Fiedler holding Johanna ("Yummy") their
first child, born September 17, 1945.

PHOTO BY DAVID WING NILSSON

Arthur Fiedler auditions Charles
Castleman, 5, for a Childrens'
Concert of The Esplanade July
17, 1946.

PHOTO BY DAVID WING NILSSON

Firebuff Fiedler shares his hobby with his Dalmatian "Sparkie."

A lasting tribute from his native city appears on a plaque at the base of the bridge named for him in 1953.

ARTHUR FIEDLER
BRIDGE

ERECTED IN 1953, THE 25th YEAR OF
THE ESPLANADE CONCERTS · NAMED IN
HONOR OF THEIR CREATOR AND CONDUCTOR
DEVOTING HIS MUSICAL GIFT TO THE SERVICE
OF THE PUBLIC IN HIS NATIVE COMMUNITY
HE HAS HERE BROUGHT MUSIC OF THE MASTERS TO
COUNTLESS THOUSANDS IN THESE CONCERTS, THE FIRST
TO BE PLAYED EACH SUMMER BY A MAJOR SYMPHONY
ORCHESTRA FREE TO ALL.

CHRISTIAN A. HERTER
GOVERNOR

Arthur Fiedler conducts the Boston Symphony at a Friday afternoon concert on December 15, 1955 as part of his twenty-fifth anniversary year as the conductor of the Pops.

"Fire Chief" Fiedler instructs his son Peter in the use of his new hook and ladder while sisters "Yummy" and Debbie look on with Mother (circa 1954).

Harold L. Zellerbach (left), President of the San Francisco Art Commission, and Mayor George Christopher welcome the conductor's return in 1958.

PHOTO BY GEORGE SHIMMON

Josefa Heifitz prepares to perform as guest soloist on a
Fiedler San Francisco Pops program in August 1958.

In the garden of their Brookline home the Fiedlers welcome Papa back from a concert tour in the Spring of 1960.
From left, Peter, Ellen, the Maestro, Johanna and Deborah.

More than 10,000 people attended a Sunday afternoon concert at Stern Grove

of the Bottomley brothers would cooperate by waiting
up somewhere to come in with sister, so that Mother
Bottomley need not be disturbed by the frequency of her
daughter's rendezvous with the fascinating director.

When the Junior League Players presented "The
Prince Who Was A Pauper" at various charitable insti-
tutions, Ellen as "Maid-in-waiting" always had her eye
on the Fiedler baton. She was pictured in the social columns among the bathing beauties at the Gay Nineties
Pops Concert. Her striking appearance was bait to columnists . . . "in a gown of red that sweeps the floor, cut
low in the neck to show her gleaming shoulders," or
"glimpsed in sunrise pink velvet with a spray of garde-
nias on her shoulder and sleeves of golden brown just
matching her eyes." Arthur's penetrating eyes must have
drunk in those pictures, too, as his presence was usually
noted at important social affairs.

It was not Ellen, however, who won the waltz competition with the master of waltz conductors at a December benefit for the Christopher Shop. Nancy Morrison,
"adorable in pale pink tulle over pink taffeta" danced off
with that honor. In fact, the future Mrs. Fiedler was so
discreet that her hundreds of competitors were almost as
ignorant of the deepening romance as was her mother.

They continued to elude the columnists to such an
extend that in the summer of 1936, the "Post" commented that "Arthur Fiedler, than whom there is no
greater social success, has a small runabout, but likely as

not it is apt to be driven by one of his innumerable lovely lady admirers. After a concert like his, a virtuoso needs rest and a charming chauffeur is no little help."

Such printed "compliments" did not help to build up the Fiedler image in the mind of Koussevitzky. Nor did his published portrait as a "Man of Distinction" on a nation-wide whiskey advertisement! But the real step over the boundary had to do with music.

One winter season, Hotel Ritz-Carlton management approached Fiedler with the suggestion that he bring a group of Symphony players to entertain Sunday evening diners. Arthur Fiedler's public is never classified. He will make music wherever he has an audience. Applause from a dining tycoon is just as welcome as praise from a city laborer who stops him on the street to thank him for playing Puccini on the Esplanade. He accepted the hotel's offer as energetically as he picked up a proffered baton thirty years later when an ex-symphony player in San Francisco asked him if he would like to conduct the dance orchestra at Station "J"—a newly-opened semi-night club.

Word of the Ritz-Carlton project reached the conductor of the Boston Symphony Orchestra. He came to the Monday morning rehearsal looking wan.

"I hear," he said, looking across the hall at Fiedler, who had stopped by enroute to the music library, "that some of you are playing where zay eat. It makes me ill!" He clutched his stomach, as he turned to the Concert Master, "Burgin, take the stick. I'm going home."

There were many among the Boston critics who did not understand the continual snubbing of their favorite young Pops conductor by the illustrious Russian. Such writers reflected a growing sentiment among influential symphony goers, like the Fullers and Bottomleys, that Arthur Fiedler should be invited to be a guest conductor. These people who knew him best appreciated the studious hours that lay behind his well-chosen programs. They watched his patience with younger aspirants for fame and listened to the talks on music which he gave in museums and art galleries, as well as over the air.

Year after year Mrs. Bottomley and Ellen attended every concert he gave. They always occupied front row balcony seats at the Pops, or sat together at The Esplanade. Mrs. Bottomley had never forgotten the musical pleasures of her early widowhood when she had sat quietly in the presence of two highly sensitive and accomplished performers who forgot everything else in their effort toward perfection. She was glad that her well-traveled daughter also appreciated good music, and grateful for Ellen's stimulating companionship. But still she was unaware of the inner communication that focused the girl's attention on every motion of the man on the podium.

Each summer as they mingled with the crowds on The Esplanade Ellen became more sensitive to the magnetism that attracted Boston to the plucky musician who had defied her "Uncle Allie's" scorn of untried concerts by the river. Possessive pride in her friend's accomplishments made his success her own. Quietly, and as far as possible out of sight of snooping columnists, their romance deepened, like others nourished under the spell of moonlit concerts.

Their marriage, in January, 1942, during the early weeks of World War II, made exciting headlines in Boston's society columns. Like the music he was blending into concerts to unify the divergent elements in the city's population, Fiedler's choice of bride made him more wholly theirs. Ellen's lineage tied her to early America; her dedicated Catholic faith, to the growing majority in this city founded by Pilgrims. Between them they bound together all the cultural traditions of the community they both loved. Age difference was overlooked in their mutuality of interests.

But even their wedding date had been unexpectedly and hastily changed. Invitations had gone out for an early December ceremony in the great Cathedral when Ellen was struck down by a vicious streptococcus throat infection. On what would have been her wedding day, she was delirious with fever. That passed, but she was so languid and weak that she could not cope with Boston's blizzards. She was shipped off to the mountains of North Carolina with a trained nurse. Christmas came and went. Letters told her of the gay family party at the Fullers, with Arthur an acceped member of the clan. Homesick as she was, she still did not have the strength to return.

But that day had finally come. On January 5, 1942, Arthur Fiedler had applied for a wedding license, and three days later Ellen's life-long friend, Father O'Connell, had quietly married them in the rectory of the Cathedral of the Holy Cross. Still fearful that some hex might yet be on them, she had sent brother John for the bridegroom—"to be sure that he had not changed his mind, or overslept."

Like other wartime couples, their honeymoon was short. Ellen was soon using all her charm to win over the housekeeper who had so long domineered the pampered bachelor. Before the wedding Ellen had sat down with this determined lady, who had threatened to leave as soon as she had heard of the approaching change of status. Mrs. Smith was motherly under her gruff exterior. The sight of the pale girl who was about to cope with erratic schedules and exotic gourmet taste persuaded her to move with the Fiedlers to the new apartment in Brookline.

Emanuel and 'Rika, now living in Brookline, too, near to Uncle Benny and the Hochlands, soon fell under the spell of the bride, whose health returned with her happiness.

When the Pops season opened, a picture of *Mrs.* Arthur Fiedler showed her still sitting inconspicuously in the front row balcony with her mother and brother—"a charming bride in black and white print, a saucy lipstick-red hat matched by a large envelope purse."

A few months after their marriage Ellen's sympathy was needed to tide her new family over deep sorrow. Uncle Benny, who had played with the Boston Symphony for forty-five years, died in Brookline, five years after his brother Gus had been taken. Kindly, whimsical Uncle Benny had been part of Arthur's life as long as he could remember. He had harbored him as a lonely refugee from Germany in 1915, had found him a place in the orchestra and indoctrinated him into the secrets of the organization. Through all the twelve years that he had played under his nephew in the Pops, fierce family pride had flared if ever a word of criticism was aimed at the conductor. But ordinarily he was unemotional, and made light of the younger Fiedler's authority. One day in a Pops rehearsal Benny's seatmate was disturbed when Fiedler noticed a wrong note.

"Oh, never mind," consoled the uncle. "It's only Arthur . . . not Koussevitzky."

Emanuel, the eldest, was now the only remaining Fiedler violinist of his generation. He kept telling Ellen that for two hundred years there had been a direct line of fine musicians in their family. With longing eyes, he held out empty arms.

"I want grandchildren," he would say. "What's the matter?"

"Why don't you talk to your son?" came back the quick reply. Ellen was fond of her father-in-law. She shared his oft-expressed yearning.

But he did not live to hold the little Johanna who was born on September 17, 1945, the first child in this Fiedler generation—beautiful like her grandmother, whose name she bears.

Arthur's late friend Charles O'Connell, in his book "The Other Side of the Record," remarked that with the coming of the baby, Fiedler's father instincts were diverted from his collection of tropical fish, which he now left to an automatically-controlled aquarium. He noted the contrast between Fiedler's famous irritation with sharp or flat vibrations and his attuning himself to the new baby's crying, but also credited the latter as perhaps the reason that the Pops was playing at its best.

It was not long before the apartment was outgrown, and Louise Smith decided that she could not make the adjustment even if her employer could. She left Ellen with her book of Arthur's favorite recipes and departed before the family moved into the large brick house at 133 Hyslop Road in Brookline. Here black-eyed Deborah was born—to join the sister whose difficult name she shortened to "Yummy" as soon as she could make herself understood. Almost simultaneously with the birth of this second child, the household was enlarged by a gentle French-Canadian named Celia, whose function ranges from nurse to caretaker, and without whose backstage presence no Fiedler would know where to turn.

The two girls had passed the kindergarten stage before the family was rounded out with the birth of a son. They called the little image of his father "Peter" and began to make plans for a fireside ensemble of their own in years to come.

Peter's babyhood was difficult. He seemed to have

inherited more than good looks from his father. The strings on this "fiddler" were tight strung and the baby stomach regurgitated almost every experimental food. One night, after an especially trying session, Ellen stood at the nursery door holding a spotless small boy all snapped into his "Dr. Denton's." The Maestro stepped out of his room, resplendent in meticulously tailored tails, his stiffly starched shirt glistening. He could not resist the angelic smile. Spontaneously, he hugged the tiny form, and tears overflowed his own eyes as he gently laid his son in the waiting crib. Ellen stood on the other side, and their hands touched in humble contemplation of the miracle their love had wrought. No one in Symphony Hall that night could have guessed why in the *Siegfried Idyll* he "made the music sound like the intimate and precious gift bestowed by Wagner on his Cosima . . . never was music more lighted by an inner and tender glow of rejoicing emotion."

Wagner had his Triebschen with its stately poplars and the distant view of Lake Lucerne. Within the confines of this park he found detachment—and love. Across the world, in Brookline, one of his modern interpreters also looks from his window into tree tops and as far as possible closes his door on a vast admiring public when he steps into the trophy-filled hallway of his three-story home.

The sign, "Mr. Fiedler," on the door of the conductor's studio-wing in this large house was snitched in his youth from a dressing room in some far off city. In its transplanted setting, as in its original place, it became an effective barrier against intrusion. Once behind its protection, nothing short of a fire alarm could disturb him. The toy fire engine on the fireplace mantel, brought to him by one of his orchestra members from a European toyshop, symbolized this avocation. Otherwise, his "castle" became increasingly music-centered, its bookcases filled with biographies of great conductors and his world-famous collection of miniature scores. Here, among his files of rare and current recordings, the precious mementos of his Camden trip found permanent place; and he learned from the greatest of contemporary and recently-deceased conductors as he played and replayed their finest recordings. Many a time, as he could listen again to the precise tempo of a Karl Muck record, the Pops Conductor would express gratitude that it was still possible to learn indefinitely from "a man with such vital power."

As the young Fiedlers grew from babyhood, their father's hours downstairs in the gum-paneled library were more frequent. He regretted the long absences from home required by his profession, knowing that bringing up a family should not be a mother's task alone, and he set aside the before-dinner hour to sink into his easy chair and listen to the day's events in the lives of his children. Like his father and mother, he expected and required much from these three, the only descendants to carry on the two-century-old "fiddler" name. Practicing became as definite a part of their daily routine as it had been in the Boston and Berlin homes of their father. They all showed talent at an early age, although no one of them seemed single-mindedly attached to music. Rarely some privileged friend heard the result of this practice on the grand piano in the drawing room—one of four instruments scattered about the large home, along with the seven Hi-Fi sets that made listening to recordings an integral part of daily living.

Long ago this exacting man, who demanded excellence in all things from his family as from his orchestra, learned that "privacy is the secret of a happy home." The staccato of "company voices" seldom interrupted the quieting adagio of the Fiedler home as the man who came to symbolize perpetual motion on podiums everywhere returned to recharge his batteries in the free hours left for home and family.

Those hours became fewer as the world demanded more from Arthur Fiedler; but when he had a few weeks between guest conducting, yearly tours, recordings and auditions, he made the most of his quiet home routine. His little Volkswagon chugged up to Symphony Hall with the punctuality of a time-clock. Morning hours passed swiftly, between rehearsals, studying scores, and meticulous answering of letters. His secretary's phone call to Ellen at one-forty-five—"He has left."—assured a hearty meal waiting in Brookline. Ellen mastered the art of tasteful goulash and a well-flavored salad—always without dressing—as soon as she inherited Louise Smith's cookbook!

After that the closed door to the studio wing meant that silence reigned until Papa came out in late afternoon to take Sparky—his black-spotted Dalmatian—for a walk. A light supper, a short family hour in the library, and then he must dress and be off to a concert.

The world image of Arthur Fiedler—exhilarating, never-aging conductor—would hardly recognize this home-loving "papa"; but his children accepted both aspects with equanimity. At the age of six, "Yummy" was visiting friends in Oakland, California, who took her, Debbie, and some other youngsters to the Children's Fairyland. Her hostess dropped a dime in the music box in front of *Goldie Locks and the Three Bears*.

"My God! It's Fiedler," solemnly declared the little girl as the record began.

Some seventeen years later this eldest daughter—enrolled for the second year in Bowdoin College Summer Music School in Maine—was playing in the viola section of an orchestra led by her father at a concert for the benefit of the scholarship fund of the college.

"This will be the first time I have ever played for papa," Johanna told a "Boston Globe" reporter prior to the concert. "I always make a point of practicing when he's not in the house; but I know that he will be fair. I've watched him conduct other members of our family, and he never separated them from the other musicians."

Thus this Sarah Lawrence College Senior, heretofore an accomplished pianist, acknowledged to her father that she wanted to be the third generation of Fiedlers playing under him—by perfecting her command of his own favorite instrument.

Debbie, the younger sister, at Radcliffe, carried on another family tradition by diverting from piano to 'cello, as her Aunt Rosa had done, to be ready for her turn to play in an orchestra under Arthur Fiedler.

"Papa's" insistence on *practice* made good pianists out of all three of his children, but Peter's choice of an auxiliary instrument—the steel guitar—hardly pointed to an orchestra seat. It did, however, bring his agile father to the dance floor at Debbie's debut in 1965 when Peter and two other 'teen-agers assembled a combo to supplement part-time for the professional orchestra.

"Your tempo is not fast enough," shouted the Maestro. Forgetting his childhood chagrin when his own father had tuned his violin on the stage of the Boston Latin School, Father Fiedler grabbed Peter's baton and led the boys to a fury. Then he passed it back to his son, as he tagged a long-haired blonde and started frugging with an intensity that sent his silver mane flying and brought sweat to pour from his dripping face for the rest of the evening.

CHAPTER EIGHT

Military Marches Again

WHEN ESPLANADE CONCERTS began in the war-jittery summer of 1942, Boston's Civil Defense authorities panicked. They looked at the brilliantly-lighted Shell with hundreds of people spread out on the grassy bank and shuddered to think of the target offered for any possible enemy sub or plane. Such large conspicuous public gatherings were against all rules of safety!

Fiedler himself was half-convinced. He called in Lanny Humphrey. . . . "Send out some press releases. We'll have to stop the concerts."

Then an avalanche of letters heaped on his Symphony Hall desk. The phone rang incessantly there and at home. "Special Deliveries" arrived at all hours. Fiedler's eyes raced through plea after plea. They came from Boston music-lovers and from servicemen in every branch. A war bride wrote: "Please, Mr. Fiedler, keep on playing. I can never thank you enough for that music on The Esplanade. Memories of those evenings Joe and

125

I had together under the stars are very precious now that
he has gone."

"Gosh, Lanny," Fiedler tossed the letter to his
friend. "If this means so much, we'll have to find a way!"

The Metropolitan District Commissioners backed
them in a compromise. Concerts were played earlier without need of illumination, and romance seemed to flourish
in twilight as well as by the moon. In fact, the "Boston
Globe" comment, "guess you could say that Hatch Shell
has hatched a good bit of romance," became as true for
hundreds in those audiences as for its conductor. Soldiers
and sailors waiting at the Port of Boston for embarcation
orders met their girls on The Esplanade; words whispered under cover of sounds reverberating from the teak-
lined Shell often led to the altar.

In the same mood in which he had given courage
to the depressed of the 'thirties, now Arthur Fiedler was
helping to raise the morale of those who were to fight the
battles of the 'forties. Uniformed trainees streamed out
of the halls of M.I.T. and Harvard across the river. Some
stretched on the grass, exhausted by long hours of ex-
ploring the secrets of radar and sonar. Others spread
books beside them and concentrated on their logistic
problems while soothing harmonies relaxed their
tensions.

This was not, however, the war service that the
Pops Maestro had visioned after the fateful news from
Pearl Harbor on December 7, 1941. He recognized that
a man nearing fifty was too old for active service; but he

remembered Sousa's contribution to the morale of the marching men of 1917. Perhaps he could assume that role in 1941. He took his idea to his companion of the Haiti excursion, Philip Clark, now Navy Procurement Officer for Massachusetts. Clark wrote a long letter to Washington detailing Fiedler's qualifications. But their hopes were dashed by the reply saying that in such a different kind of war there would be no need for the kind of duty Sousa had performed.

While he was increasingly sensitive about his civilian status, Fiedler accepted every opportunity to help on the home front. The N.Y.A. orchestra was of course disbanded when war caused the whole Youth Administration project to be abandoned; but wherever his uniformed young musicians went, they were still his concern. And new ones came under his jurisdiction as the Mayor appointed him to the Boston Soldiers' and Sailors' Recreation Commission. The Downtown Center for Servicemen was soon echoing with serious music as Fiedler organized symphonic jam sessions for all who could play instruments of any kind—with stands, music, and instruments provided by the city. Fear and homesickness dissolved in the excitement of these "musical reading sessions" where professional trombonists and high school percussionists responded to the baton of the amiable Pops leader. Ellen Fiedler learned early to fill her own evenings while her bridegroom gave unstintedly to the boys who wore the colors.

Just as he had established The Esplanade to satisfy

public yearning for good music, so now he welcomed
every opportunity to provide worthy musical entertainment for this sudden influx of uprooted youth. When
thirty-five members of the Boston Symphony volunteered
to give a concert for servicemen at the Museum of Art,
Arthur Fiedler was the conductor. The full symphony
under Koussevitzky toured every Massachusetts Army
camp and Navy base in the state; but the busy Maestro
often called on Assistant Conductor Burgin or the Pops
Conductor to substitute for him. Thus Arthur found
himself back at Camp Devens, where he would have been
unrecognizable to that medical officer who had so
brusquely commanded him to "get out!" in 1917.

Memories of that earlier conflict also returned
when Percy Grainger precipitated violent discussion over
the question of banning for the duration the music of
all enemy composers, living or dead. "Music is international," asserted Fiedler, recalling the bitterness of
Muck's imprisonment and the suspicious attitude that
had plagued his own summer in Rockport. But he did
oppose presenting music by living German composers
when royalties would go to Nazis!

Fiedler's help was sought by Koussevitzky on a project that called for surrender of Boston Symphony's *own*
royalty rights on some recordings in order to stretch the
purchasing power of a fund raised through the orchestra's generosity. The senior Maestro was sure that homesick young people craved more than jazz. Accordingly,
he stipulated that one-half of the proceeds from a war

benefit concert at Tanglewood should go toward purchase of Boston Symphony classical recordings—and
where needed, phonographs on which to play them—in
U.S.O. Clubs and Veterans' hospitals all over Massachusetts. By arrangement with the RCA-Victor Company it
was possible to buy more at the lower cost obtained by
giving up royalties. A questionnaire was then sent to all
possible recipients to determine if they had facilities
where servicemen could listen undisturbed to good recordings; their need for phonographs and public address
equipment; and the men's choices of records. Then Koussevitzky turned to the man whose knack for arranging
programs of proved audience appeal and artistic balance
was so well known.

Fiedler piled the answers to this questionnaire beside his red leather reference book and undertook the
difficult task of deciding what to send where. "Sea chests"
of special design and color were packed according to his
plan, each containing enough records to provide ten
hour-long programs. He chose twelve complete symphonies and concertos for every chest, in addition to several
dozen discs, a typical selection including Berlioz' *Roman
Carnival Overture*, Brahms' *Fourth Symphony*, Pierne's
Entrance of the Little Fauns, the *C-Sharp Minor* concerto by Rachmaninoff, and Wolf-Ferrari's *Jewels of the
Madonna*. He was well rewarded when a letter came re-
porting that "a number of the boys told us that the one
thing they did miss in the Army was this type of music
and asked to extend the program for two hours so that

they could also play the Beethoven *Fifth,* Ravel's *Bolero,* and *Waltzes* by Johann Strauss."

Fiedler's interest in providing good music for servicemen went further. He was constantly seeking talent and creativity among young Americans wherever he went. When a former Symphony Hall usher, Carleton Breyer, put together an orchestral arrangement of *Deep in the Heart of Texas* in 1942, Fiedler gave it prominence at the Pops. Later the young man wrote a war song of his own—*The 21st Marines.* Fiedler liked it well enough to play it on a radio program so that it could be heard by Breyer's brother-in-law (to whom it was dedicated) in an Armed Services Overseas Broadcast somewhere in the South Pacific.

Actually, even the enemy was using Fiedler-led Pops concerts as propaganda, thus furnishing nostalgic entertainment for American boys in that distant combat area. "The Musician" for October, 1944, carried a picture of Fiedler on its cover, with an inside story saying, "The Japs have been so accommodating as to pick up his Saturday night concerts and relay them to our fighting men all over the Pacific area—than which only one thing could be more welcome; and that is to have their transmitter and the island on which it stands taken over by Americans."

These broadcasts, with "Tokyo Rose" as announcer, had an unexpected long-range result. The name of Fiedler and his stirring music was made so familiar in the Orient that in the peaceful era of the 'sixties he became one of Nippon's favorite conductors and even an Honorary Chief of the Tokyo Fire Department!

By 1944 Fiedler had finally found a place where his "civies" could be replaced by a uniform, if only as a Reservist in the U.S. Coast Guard. Whenever he was called, the usually correctly-tailored Maestro donned dungarees and scrubbed the decks of vessels in Boston Harbor with all the vigor of conducting a Brahms' *Allegro;* but when the Pops season closed that year the conductor appeared in dress uniform—by order of the commanding officer of the U.S.C.G. Later in the summer, sixty thousand people on The Esplanade cheered white-clad Coxswain Fiedler, again ordered to appear in dress uniform, as Coast Guard Night was observed on the bank of the Charles.

Although his offer to become the "Sousa of World War II" had been turned down, he was now leading the Coast Guard Band at many an exciting War Bond, Red Cross, or Victory Rally. Soon he was functioning as a member of Boston's Victory Concerts Committee. When this organization presented a group of Boston Symphony players under the Fiedler baton in the Boston Garden with Gracie Allen as guest soloist, a reviewer commented that "Fiedler's usually neat pompadour was considerably mussed in the fury of directing a lot of real musicians trying to play up to Gracie's musical madness; but the courtly kiss he planted on Gracie's hand was so continental that Gracie, to the delight of the audience, came back for another."

The TV star's *Concerto for Index Finger* was a successful hoax. Advance publicity had credited Gracie with special coaching by Sanromá for this appearance. Actually, Leo Litwin was performing at the piano directly beneath her, keeping his eye on Conductor Fiedler through a window cut in the floor of the platform.

When final Victory news broke on August 14, 1945, Coxswain Arthur Fiedler "on part-time duty without pay" was enjoying a bit of shore leave with Ellen and friends on the North Shore. Guest-conductor Paul Cherkassky was directing The Esplanade that night, while Harvard Professor G. Wallace Woodworth, leader of the Harvard-Radcliff Choral Society, had taken over the Monday evening concert for him. Fiedler was due back the next morning for the Children's Concert and to conduct the closing program of the season in the evening.

Esplanade Public Relations Director Laning Humphrey called Governor Tobin's secretary. "You are planning a Victory celebration, I presume."

"Yes, we are working on it," the Secretary replied.

"Well, here is an idea and we'll have to work fast to accomplish it. Tomorrow is the final concert on The Esplanade for this summer. Fiedler is out of town, but he is scheduled to conduct that. I'll get hold of him as soon as possible. He'll work up an appropriate program. We'll make this the most impressive occasion Boston has ever enjoyed."

The Secretary asked him to hold the wire until he

could consult the Governor. "Mr. Tobin says that's almost too quick," he reported. "Couldn't we get the orchestra together a day or two later?"

"Impossible!" Humphrey was emphatic. "The men all have summer jobs. They'll be scattering here, there, and everywhere. It's tomorrow or never!"

The Governor acquiesced. Humphrey found out where Fiedler was and soon had him on the phone. He sketched the plan briefly, adding, "You better come right on in. We need you to pull it all together."

"Please," Fiedler demurred. "This is vacation—the first Ellen and I have had. Don't break into it. I'll be on hand tomorrow in time for the Children's Concert. You go ahead with whatever is necessary until I get there."

"No," insisted Humphrey. "This is vital. You *must* come now!"

It was past intermission time at The Esplanade when Fiedler walked into the Shell. Cherkassky, whose only son had been killed in action in Italy earlier in the year, was overcome with emotion. He caught sight of the Maestro in the passage way, and beckoned him to the podium, handing him the baton to conduct the *Finale* of Beethoven's *Victory Symphony*. Thus caught up in the exhilaration of that night, Fiedler's agile mind was already building up a program for the morrow.

Humphrey found the conductor at the Shell early the next morning. He was scanning the pages of the red leather program book, compiling a sequence to fit the exultant mood. That posed a new problem. How were they to get these programs printed in time for the evening performance?

They put a call through to the Symphony Hall printers. A surprised voice answered. "The place is closed. I just came by to pick up something. This is a holiday, you know, by President Truman's orders."

"Couldn't you call the owners? Surely he has someone on his force willing to do this as a public service."

The answer was firmly, "no!" Fiedler knew the resourcefulness of his publicity man. There must be some way to accomplish this. "Yes," replied Humphrey, "all newspapers have job printers to do emergency work. I'll try that angle."

He began with "The Christian Science Monitor." By good fortune he had Editor Erwin Canham on the phone. "Surely," Canham replied, "we'll find a way to do it. How many will you need?"

Humphrey relayed the question to Fiedler. All three knew that the crowds would be tremendous. Canham sugested that they could make runs of four at a time, to be cut in strips. Also, they could deliver them in relays as they came off the press. In a few minutes the editor called back. He had found a printer who had volunteered out of patriotism. They had located a cut of the official seal of the Commonwealth. Soon the printer himself was on the phone. As Fiedler read off the selections, Humphrey dictated spelling and punctuation by wire. There was no time for proof reading!

In the meantime the Governor prepared an opening address. Spot announcements on the radio all day alerted the excited city. When Humphrey approached the Shell in early evening, traffic officers were already coping with surging thousands. At the back entrance they whistled him on; but he protested, "I *work* here," and he pointed to the piles of programs on the seat of his car. The officers relented and he dashed ahead of the assembling players to distribute the first installment of programs.

As the setting sun glowed red behind the white-columned Institute of Technology and blue faded out of the evening sky, the strains of *The Star Spangled Banner* echoed across The Charles. Choked voices joined in singing *America* as Fiedler motioned the audience to participate. Sousa's *The Stars and Stripes Forever* was followed by the *Finale* from *Symphony No. 5* by Shostakovitch in tribute to the fighting forces in Russia. Then Gould's *New China March* and *Knightsbridge* from the *London Suite* by Eric Coates honored those two Allies.

Governor Tobin had suggested that there should be a religious number in addition to *America*. In compliance with his request, the second half of the program commenced with *Old Hundred,* thundering out of the new electric organ recently given for the Shell by former Governor Fuller. Childish soprano blended with the husky tremolos of aging altos and basses as the vast assembly sang *Praise God From Whom All Blessings Flow.* Then people dropped back onto the grass to listen to a

French number—*Agnus Dei* (Intermezzo) from *L'Arlé-sienne Suite No. 2* by Bizet. Leo Litwin stepped to the grand piano to play typical Americana—*Rhapsody in Blue*—and the concert ended in high gear with *Salute to our Fighting Forces,* arranged by Bodge. From *The Halls of Montezuma* to *God Bless America,* marching songs of all the forces were woven into the stirring medley, sending a thankful people home, each humming some familiar air.

The next morning Humphrey called "The Monitor" to ask for the printing bill. "That," said Canham, "was our privilege—our contribution to the spirit of a grateful nation."

CHAPTER NINE

❧ ～❧

Millions in the Audience

THROUGH GUEST CONDUCTING, radio, TV, and recordings, Fiedler's audience expanded into millions, giving him perhaps more listeners than any other symphony leader in the world. Even in a small Norwegian village an old lady exclaimed, "That's America!" when the Oslo station played a Fiedler recording on its Music Hour. The man whose name was thus becoming almost synonymous with *The Stars and Stripes Forever* consistently includes on every program some such number symbolic of his devotion to the land of his birth and success.

From the beginning of The Esplanade Concerts, *The Star Spangled Banner* was always played at the beginning of the second half of the program, so that the dignity of its performance would not be interrupted by late comers. One night a mocking sneer penetrated the expected reverence of the singing audience. Fiedler's acute ear traced the sound to a young man lounging near the stage. After the last note rang out the conductor sprang down the steps and grabbed the youth by the shoulders.

"You ought to be ashamed of yourself," Fiedler shouted in tones loud enough to resound in the audience.

"What did I do?" blurted the astonished young man.

"I'll tell you what you did! You insulted our National Anthem, and you insulted the flag on the stage in front of you. Don't you ever do such a thing again. Don't you ever forget what a wonderful country it's your damned good fortune to live in!"

Fiedler's influence on the musical literacy of the United States grew as he participated in the evolution of the recording industry, dating from that first symphonic record made under Muck in 1917. His own first Boston Pops venture came in 1935 when they made a ten-inch disc recording of two gay numbers—*The Continental* from the film *The Gay Divorcee* paired with *Carioca* from the movie *Flying Down to Rio*.

Actually, records of the country's pioneering recording company—RCA-Victor—show the name "Arthur Fiedler" listed longer than any other person on the books of any such company. Recurring "firsts" offered by the Pops highlight that list, among them the recorded premier of Sanromá's performance of *Rhapsody in Blue,* and Walter Piston's *The Incredible Flutist*—written by this Harvard professor in response to Fiedler's request for a piece appropriate to Ballet Night at The Pops.

Another "first" by Fiedler was commemorated by a

framed gold disc in recognition of the first "million sale" of a semi-classical record in RCA-Victor history. Behind that memento in the Hyslop Road library wall is a typical Fiedler story. It happened in the early 'thirties that Fiedler was indulging one of his favorite whims—searching for unique items in old record and music shops. In the New York store he was sorting through a bundle of tattered sheet music when he came across a forgotten composition by Jacob Gade and quickly scanned its content, humming the melody as he read. Then he dashed out to some other engagement; but even as he threaded his way through noisy traffic, the haunting notes remained. As soon as his other business was completed he returned to the shop, found the music again, bought it, and took it to his Pops arranger. *Jalousie* became a smash hit as soon as it was put on a Boston Pops recording, and every player under his baton thereafter knew that he must learn the melody which would not leave the conductor's mind as he left the musty New York shop.

Some years later Arthur Fiedler had a call from a bearded Dane, who introduced himself as Gade, saying that he had come to Boston on a freighter to thank the Maestro for making him famous. Then the visitor opened a briefcase bulging with musical manuscripts. Fiedler searched diligently; but *Jalousie* had no worthy sequel!

Within ten years after their first listing, the Boston Pops Symphony had made six hundred recordings, with royalties topping those of Koussevitzky and the parent

Symphony. The smiling face that had won Fiedler a place among other "Men of Distinction" was pictured on so many jackets that he could no longer browse incognito, checking on record shop sales or hunting for another *Jalousie*. Nor could he travel without recognition.

In the summer of 1940, vacationing Arthur Fiedler stepped off a hot train in the volcanic mountains of Guatemala. Passengers from another train coming from the opposite direction joined the group already in the lunch room. One of them held up a Guatemala City paper, picturing the likeable man in their midst as "The Conductor of the Boston Symphony Orchestra." Cheers resounded as the proprietor produced *Jalousie* to play on a wheezing gramophone!

This misconception in the public mind which led so many times to indentification of Fiedler with the Boston *Symphony* Orchestra rather than the *Pops* began with the sale in Britain of the original Pops recording under the title—*Boston Promenade Concerts, Arthur Fiedler Conducting*. The impact of the title was so lasting that twenty years later when the Boston Symphony Orchesra appeared in London on its European Tour, British musicians inquired reproachfully—"But where is Arthur Fiedler?" An indignant listener later in Amsterdam wrote the management, asking "How come that Fiedler didn't come to lead the Boston Symphony here?"

Fiedler laughed off such stories when Laning Humphrey relayed them to him. But he always appreciated the publicity value of recordings. "Musical performances are thus made accessible the world over," he once remarked, "and it works two ways. You can remain geographically stationary and find yourself being performed far away. Then, being well known through records you find that you are frequently called upon to follow up with personal appearances."

Eventually these personal appearances brought him to podiums all over the United States and Canada, and in many foreign cities. Yet in the beginning it took dedicated cooperation and unreserved enthusiasm to win busy American listeners. When the recording company sought to make 1941 its "Greatest Year" in a campaign to bring more records into American homes, Fiedler and Eugene Ormandy sacrificed royalties on a twin gift offer. Fiedler's side presented *Ballet Music from Faust,* described by him as "melodious music which flows along a bow beautifully" as he asserted that "this gift record idea will encourage people to listen who have never considered a classical record library."

Seemingly inexhaustible Fiedler energy flowed into record promotion as it had into The Cecilia, The Pops, and The Esplanade. A Boston Society of Recorded Music elected Arthur Fiedler as President in 1948. The next year Irving Kolodin wrote in the "New York Sun" that "Fiedler's feeling for period music is a long-familiar fact resulting indeed in some of the most delightful records in this country. The period does not matter so long as there is style inherent in the music; he is likely to seek it out and make it live again. We have rarely heard him do anything with the care, taste, and incisiveness that he applies to these minor masterpieces." (four Auber overtures).

Boston Pops recordings headed the list of "101 Best Sellers" in the classical and semi-classical category when RCA-Victor totalled public response in 1953, even though the competition included Toscanini and the NBC Orchestra. Three years later the revised list of "All-Time Best Sellers" found Fiedler's orchestra still leading, with sixteen selections. Among them, *Waltzes of the Strauss Family,* made the Boston Pops the best-selling American orchestra in Europe. Arthur Fiedler's youthful training under Johann Strauss III shows in every swelling strain of these favorite tunes. Whether one hears them in concert hall, over the air, or from stereo speakers, their lilt brings to mind a picture of the silver-haired Pops Maestro almost waltzing himself as balance shifts from one foot to the other, his white stick pointing from first to second violins in the swinging melodies.

Among the Fiedler treasures is a gold-embossed plaque in a gold frame which was presented to the Maestro in the summer of 1959. Its words express the esteem of those who had been closest to him as he had won his world-wide audience of record-listeners:

"On the occasion of the Thirtieth Espanade Season, this plaque is presented by RCA-Victor to one of the world's outstanding ambassadors of good music, in recognition of the sale of his two-millionth album."

This two millionth album was made under conditions as strikingly different from the stifling "orange cup studio" in Camden as jet Clippers of 1959 differed from the monoplane in which Lindbergh crossed the Atlantic. Today Symphony Hall is transformed into a recording studio as modern electrical equipment is rolled into place; its perfect acoustics preserve every nuance of the conductor's interpretation.

Sometimes the orchestra members play in their regular seats on the stage. Other days half the audience chairs are removed, and the players are located so as to produce sound effects needed for stereo. In another room the representative of the recording company listens to a speaker, with a direct phone connecting to the podium. A light flashes a warning, and Fiedler stops to hear the man who has listened to the oral image on tape say, "the brass is a little heavy" or "the piccolo is a trifle shrill."

Intermission brings no rest for conductor and listener. While players lounge in the Green Room, or smoke in the doorways, Fiedler and Peter Delheim—or whoever happens to represent the recording company that season—play back the tape, discuss its merits or defects, and perhaps decide to re-do a section when they re-assemble. Since modern tapes can be spliced, there is no need for the long tedious repetitions of early days.

Fiedler has built his reputation on such endless patience and attention to detail; and his wide knowledge of instruments and the people who play them gives au-

thentic amosphere to anything selected for these albums.
One day a Jamaica rumba was to be included. Delheim
protested that the tempo was too slow.

"No," asserted Fiedler, "I was there. That is the
way the natives play it."

Sometimes the conductor furnishes the "atmosphere." Engineers and orchestra gathered for the first
recording of an arrangement of Western songs from TV
to be known as *Pops Round-Up* were not unduly surprised when Fiedler walked in wearing a ten-gallon hat!
Rhythmic dance music is apt to be illustrated with feet
as well as hands. Be it mazurka or waltz, tango or twist,
Fiedler, versatile and agile, is familiar with the latest
craze.

Opening night of a Broadway musical usually finds
Fiedler in the audience, his ear alert for catchy tunes.
Pops recordings have carried the melodies of Gershwin,
Bernstein, and Richard Rodgers as far into the ether as
disc jockeys spin platters. A Fiedler-led recording became the only symphonic version of *No Strings* soon
after he heard the opening of this Rodgers show, and
called in his arrangers to orchestrate the tuneful score
with strings.

Familiarity with Fiedler style has been acquired
through many media in addition to recordings. First on
radio, and later on such TV programs as *Great Music
From Chicago, The Firestone Hour,* and the *Ed Sullivan
Show,* Pops tempo has resounded in family rooms across
the nation.

Beginning with the night in 1926 when WEEI allowed radio listeners to catch the enthusiasm of Fiedler's first conducting of the Pops, he and his orchestra have transmitted stimulating music over the airwaves. The Sinfonietta—whose name he wisely copyrighted at the beginning—made its radio debut on February 28, 1927; and The Esplanade concerts were broadcast by WNCA in the second season—for one-half hour every Tuesday and Friday evening. This continued until Depression deprived the orchestra of a sponsor in 1932. During that time, "Program Notes by Arthur Fiedler" enlivened the Radio Page of the "Boston Sunday Herald," winning audiences by his subtle humor and his knowledge of music and composers.

In Fiedler's opinion broadcasting inspires players to their best. A restless or apathetic audience in a hall disturbs the performers. But there is a mysterious lilt to the excitement of the studio. "Who knows what great conductor may be in that unseen audience?" he said, as Esplanade players prepared to go on the air in the early 'thirties. "Perhaps Stokowski, or even Toscanini may be listening to us."

He often compares a program maker to a good chef. "He must have the right amount of thickening and spice—a generous dash of 'good music.' Perhaps it will be a Bach or Handel suite, a Ravel tone-poem in addition to the expected popular numbers. Broadcasts build up appreciation for fine symphonic concerts."

Boston came to recognize Fiedler's gourmet taste

in music as in food. Sponsors were found to present the
Pops over the air on Monday evenings; and by the early
'forties his *Sundays-at-four-thirty* were an anticipated
part of WBZ's regular fare. Here, as at Pops and Esplanade, he used exceptionally talented young artists as
guests. Auditions for these radio debuts cut deeply into
his time. Thirty-three vocalists appeared in one day before a panel of the leading Boston music critics and
Arthur Fiedler; the next day the same group listened to
twenty-eight instrumentalists. In one two-week interval,
they passed judgment on nearly five hundred young musicians. There seemed to be no limit to Fiedler interest
in aspiring performers. He even agreed to conduct an
"orchestra" of fifty spinets at a Boston Piano Fair, where
a partially paralyzed girl from Salem so intrigued him
with her ingenuity that he detained her afterward to
learn how she had re-arranged hundreds of classics to be
played with right hand alone.

While all this activity was claiming Fiedler's attention in Boston, he was the unknowing subject of a discussion in San Francisco, which eventually made him a
cross-continent commuter. A group of oil executives in
that far western city were considering the choice of conductor for the coming summer programs of *The Standard Hour*. This series of Sunday evening broadcasts had
grown out of studio proportions; first, into a small downtown Club theatre, and by this time filling the War
Memorial Opera House with guests of Standard Oil
Company of California—to furnish "live" applause for

programs heard over the air in the far western states. During the fall and winter, opera and symphony had been presented, with guest artists from the current seasons. A succession of differing personalities had conducted lighter programs each of the past few summers. Discussion of a leader for the coming months had reached an impasse when Program Manager Adrian Michaelis exclaimed,

"Well, if we are really going to put on a pops series, why not engage Mr. Pops himself—Arthur Fiedler!"

"Oh, you'll never get him out of Boston!" protested a musically-knowledgeable member of the committee.

It was worth a try. Michaelis started negotiations through a local talent agent. Before he knew the outcome, one of Standard's music-loving executives had occasion to visit friends in Boston.

"How would you like to spend an evening at the Pops?" asked their hosts. The Howard Vespers accepted with alacrity, their interest heightened when the Bostonians added, "we understand that Fiedler is thinking of going out to your city this summer."

After the concert the four made their way to the Green Room, where Vesper cordiality paved the way for friendly introduction of Arthur Fiedler to what has become his "adopted city" in the years that have followed.

As a matter of fact, it did not really take much persuasion to intrigue Fiedler with an invitation to lead an

orchestra made up of men trained under Pierre Monteux, then Conductor of the San Francisco Symphony!

Ellen left the two small girls in charge of Celie and
a nurse who had been her own caretaker in early years,
and joined her husband on that first trip to the city
which two years later would institute the only successful
rival to the Boston Pops.

Those first three concerts—on July 31, August 7
and 14, 1949—were happy. H. D. Collier, then Chairman of the Board, wrote Public Relations Manager
Stewart Brown after the last one: "The thought ran
though my mind as I listened to the concert last evening
—'why not keep this man Arthur Fiedler for the summer?' I am glad to see that you have gone in for better
music and have taken our program out of the rut and
put it on the level I have been hopeful of for a long
time."

Brown replied that he had not been able to get
Fiedler for a longer period, but "he was so taken by
San Francisco that he would like to return next summer
and will let us know for how many engagements."

No one could then foresee how many return engagements that first visit would lead to, nor how many
hopeful artists of the Pacific Coast would find a creative
listener in the man who would soon do almost as much
for San Francisco as he had done for Boston.

At the conclusion of his second season as conductor
of *The Standard Hour,* Arthur Fiedler was invited by
the Board of Directors of the Bohemian Club to be a

guest at the Summer Encampment at their Grove on the Russian River. Here his conducting of the Tunerville 'cello octet unexpectedly paved the way for a new phase of his widening career. Bob Newell, honorary member of the camp orchestra, was host to the visiting conductor in his smaller camp, the *Better 'Ole,* but naturally took him at once to the musical center of the Grove, where the sudden recognition of the sour 'cello note spread intimate fame among musically-minded men of influence.

A member of the San Francisco Art Commission, Attorney John K. Hagopian, was among the amazed audience who listened to the Maestro's skillful handling of these amateurs at *Camp Bromley.* Howard Vesper, a member of *Aviary*—the Chorus camp—was also there. As the two chatted afterward, Hagopian discovered that *The Standard Hour* was to be discontinued, giving way to the inroads of TV. Both agreed that a musician now so close to the hearts of western listeners should not be lost to San Francisco.

The lawyer made a point of dropping into Newell's camp to get better acquainted with the Boston conductor. Their mutual interest in young musicians colored a fruitful conversation. Hagopian was pleased with Fiedler's account of the way interest in Pops and Esplanade had led to increased attendance by young people at the regular Boston Symphony winter series.

When he returned to San Francisco he took the idea germinated under the redwoods to his associates at the next meeting of the Art Commission. This group is entrusted with a sizeable grant of city funds to be used for the maintenance of a symphony. If they could supplement box office receipts with that sum, he was sure that they could fill the Civic Auditorium for San Francisco Pops Concerts modeled after the successful Boston series, especially when the popular conductor had already made such a host of friends through *The Standard Hour*. Moreover, Fiedler's interest in and ability to choose talented young artists would mean that they would not have to spend large sums on "names." The Art Commission concurred, and an exchange of wires to and from Boston brought Fiedler's acceptance of their offer. An agreement was reached with the San Francisco Symphony Association to hire the regular orchestra for an experimental series that proved to be exactly what the city wanted.

As plans for the series progressed Fiedler found a compatible co-worker in the Secretary of the Art Commission, Joseph A. Dyer, Jr. Here was a man who shared his own zeal for encouraging young talent and whose knowledge of promising soloists was inexhaustible. They were in complete agreement that the San Francisco Pops should offer debut opportunities for ambitious musicians growing up in or near this city where all races have mingled congenially since the Clippers first brought adventurers through the Golden Gate.

The San Francisco Pops opened with a gala performance in July, 1951. Fiedler requested that beautiful Lucine Amara return to her native city as the first guest soloist—a request that involved complicated correspond-ence between Joe Dyer and the Metropolitan Opera man-agement in New York to secure a special release for this one appearance.

The cavernous Civic Auditorium where proud San Franciscans welcomed this singer whose debut under Monteaux was still fresh in memory, could not be trans-formed into a Viennese garden like the green and gold spring-decorated Symphony Hall in Boston. But the old building—erected in 1915 for the Panama-Pacific Inter-national Exposition—was bright with flaming gladioli. Red-checked table cloths on closely-crowded tables, with candles dripping colored wax over beer-bottle holders, provided uniquely appropriate atmosphere. Maids and waiters carrying trays of beer and cokes found it increas-ingly difficult to weave their way between the merry-makers as succeeding series of Pops concerts became an institution in fog-cooled San Francisco summers. Above them steep rows of gallery seats were filled with music-lovers of all ages, who queued up for tickets twice a week. One ardent admirer of the Boston music-maker occupied the same seat directly above the stage for ten years. She liked to watch the changing expressions on the con-ductor's face!

This devotee had a prize view one night when a champagne cork shot out of a bottle being opened beside a front table. The swift missile struck a violinist in the middle of his bald pate. Fiedler beckoned with his free hand, and the player tossed the cork back to him during a rest. With the accuracy of a southpaw, the conductor pitched the cork back to the exact table whence it had come. Accompanied by a laughing audience, the concert continued without interruption.

But friends who joined the Maestro in the Green Room at the end of the program saw a different reaction Fiedler's eyes sparked anger.

"I always like fun," he said, "but that person carried it too far. He might have put out a player's eye!"

A few times during the years in which Arthur Fiedler came to be welcomed as an "adopted San Franciscan," Ellen came with him; but for the most part those summer weeks have meant return to the gregarious ways of his early Boston bachelor days. This city, bohemian since its '49-er beginning, intrigues a *bon vivant* like the Pops conductor. He became a favorite guest on Nob Hill, Pacific heights, and in St. Francis Wood; but his fondness for night prowling gave him a more intimate knowledge of the people and music of North Beach and Chinatown than that of many of his hosts.

Sleep never comes easily after an exhilarating concert. If there was no special social engagement after greeting the long line of Green Room autograph seekers, he would slip away with a bachelor-percussionist to look in on the night owls of Upper Grant Avenue. The musical twang of a guitar in "Little Italy," or the insistent plucking of a butterfly harp in a Chinese Theatre became invitations to hours of good listening. Sometimes he amazed a player by asking to take over the instrument himself.

"Listen," he would say, "you can get a better tone if you hold it this way" . . . and another seat holder for the Auditorium gallery was won.

As for the orchestra, which that convert would hear, it is not composed of so many strings, woodwinds, and percussionists. Rather, it is an assemblage of old friends, remembered for their special talents or personalities. If someone dropped out during the previous winter, Fiedler quickly asked the reason. If possible, he searched for the missing member asking him to play again with the Pops.

Rehearsal hours are always strenuous for conductor and players. A crash towel thrown over Fiedler's long-sleeved black shirt is often used to wipe sweat from a face steaming with effort. Longish hair waves with his arms as the conductor works up to a Wagnerian crescendo—sometimes revealing the balding spot usually camouflaged with brushed silver. Nerve impulses speed from brain to sensitive fingers—not long and artistic, but square and Germanic—conveying to accustomed players every musical mood their leader seeks. These musicians playing under Fiedler's baton have trained their eyes to watch, not only those hands, but also every means of communication—from lifted eyebrows to dancing toes. If he pulls his ear they know that something is wrong, and they are ready for the uplifted palm that stops them all.

One morning Rudolph Friml was watching Fiedler conduct a rehearsal of two new pieces which he had recently composed for a special presentation. As the players found their way through the manuscript pages of *Slavonic Rhapsody* and *Exodus to Hong Kong,* the eighty-year old composer stood below the platform beating time. Fiedler's back was toward him but courtesy was in every gesture, as he turned after a discord in the horns.

"This should be B-flat, not B-natural," he said with a tolerant smile, and the composer agreed.

Friml came onto the platform urging more action. Fiedler stopped for consultation. Then he picked up the baton again, as the sprightly octogenarian stood behind him, one hand clutching the concert master's shoulder while the other waved behind the Maestro with clenched fist beat.

Rarely was there a guest of Friml's maturity. The well known pattern of presenting qualified younger musicians at the Pops furnishes incentive to innumerable applicants. Even with Dyer's careful scrutiny, the list of young people hoping for a place the following year is always long by the time the Pops season begins. Not one of the hopeful performers is slighted, no matter what happens to the Maestro's schedule. A busy secretary overlooked a girl—who later gave a stunning performance on the Auditorium stage. "Tell her to come in during the noon hour," Fiedler suggested; his own meal was forgotten in the pleasure of discovering real talent.

Near the close of the 1963 season there was a typical late afternoon of auditions in the white marble Masonic Memorial Hall atop Nob Hill—where two seasons of Pops were performed while the old Auditorium was undergoing face lifting. Rehearsal had been almost continuous from nine to four, except for a lunch break. But Fiedler's attention never lagged as he sat beside Dyer, note book in hand. It was nearly seven o'clock when he smiled encouragement with his thanks to the last performer. Then, as the heavy doors closed behind the departing applicants, the conductor dropped, spread eagle, on the rising aisle ramp. "I've had it!" he exclaimed to Dyer and two friends who had sat through the long succession of try-outees.

Dyer protested, as he often did—"Why did you let them go on? You knew some of them couldn't make it after the first few measures!"

"I know," the conductor admitted, "but I just couldn't cut them off."

Fiedler's consideration for these young people has no limits. Sometimes he hears them in private auditions in his hotel suite. As soon as a girl drops her wrap on a chair he puts her at ease with pleasantries and inquires about her special musical interests. Perhaps the visitor is an awkward high school lad with a violin case under his arm. Fiedler picks up the instrument, tests the strings and hands it to the boy, saying, "Play just a bit from the last movement." Or a pianist's hands are stumbling nervously over an Allegro. Fiedler's voice is soothing. "Let's hear some of the Adagio," or "try to relax . . . don't play so heavily; cover up your weak spots."

The candidate may not be ready for public performance. "Practice some more and come to see me next
year," said with a pat on the shoulder and a smile, sends
this aspirant away undented, his head still held high.

On the other hand, Fiedler sometimes has the satisfaction of offering a hearing to an artist who has already
achieved recognition far from home. Such a one was introduced by Harold L. Zellerbach, the President of the
Art Commission, who told of meeting a young San Franciscan, Franca Duval, on shipboard enroute home from
triumphal appearances at La Scala in Milan.

"Let me give her an American debut," offered the
Pops conductor, and hundreds of proud citizens from
San Francisco's "Little Italy" poured into the summer
concert. A few years later Franca returned to solo at
Italian Night at the Pops when the celebration of the
One-Hundredth Anniversary of the unification of Italy
filled the galleries to the top thirty-cent seat with cheer-
ing admirers.

Not only members of the Art Commission, but also
the city's music critics continually bring their "finds"
to Fiedler. Alexander Fried, of the "San Franciso Exam-
iner" came home from the Summer Bach Festival in
Carmel, enthusiastic over the performance of a young
artist then almost forgotten by the public.

He called Joe Dyer, at the Art Commission office
to say, "I've just heard Ruth Slenczynska as piano soloist
at the Bach Festival, with Gastone Usigli conducting.

Why don't you ask her to play with Fiedler? She performed beautifully. I was greatly impressed!"

Dyer hesitated. "She's been out of circulation a long time."

"Yes, I know," interrupted Fried. "She has been out of the public eye lately, but people haven't forgotten that brilliant little girl and her debut at Mills College when she was only four years old. Now she plays with great virtuosity—the kind big audiences like. Her Bach at Carmel was exceptionally fine and deeply artistic in feeling."

Dyer thanked the critic and hastened to Fiedler with the news.

"Do you remember the child prodigy, Ruth Slenczynska?" he asked.

"Well, of course," Fiedler replied with evident interest. "What has become of her? She dropped out of sight years ago."

"You should hear Alexander Fried on the subject! He heard her at the Bach Festival, and you'd think he's struck a gold mine. He tells me that after her self-imposed retirement she has come back a mature virtuoso. She is just the artist we need to make our closing concert spectacular."

Fiedler was intrigued. "Tell Fried to call her up," he said. "If she wants to audition, I'll be glad to consider her."

Ruth and her husband were at breakfast in their

little Berkeley home when the phone rang. "This is Alexander Fried speaking. Would you like to play at the Pops?"

The girl whose rebellion against her demanding father had forced her to think that she had put the public out of her life forever listened incredulously as Fried continued. "Mr. Fiedler could use you at the final concert this summer, if you wish to audition. I've already talked to Joe Dyer, and he says you should call Mr. Fiedler at the Mark Hopkins Hotel right away."

The cordial voice that answered her call to the Pops Maestro presaged a friendship that not only became personal, but also that helped to bring this delightful young woman back into the public arena.

"Come right over," Arthur Fiedler said that morning in 1951. He greeted her as an old acquaintance.

"We've met before," he said, to her surprise.

"But where?"

"In Symphony Hall in 1935. You were ten years old. I went backstage to congratulate you and your father." The conductor looked approvingly at the slim young woman and laughed. "You were a pudgy little girl, but you had that Boston audience entranced. I shall never forget my excitement over your performance. You know, I have always been interested in gifted children. Now, let's hear what you are doing today."

She sat at the grand piano playing Rachmaninoff with poignant memories of childhood hours in the presence of the sad-faced composer.

Fiedler listened a few minutes and then interrupted her. "What would you like to play at The Pops?"

As they talked they found their tastes congenial. She went back to Berkeley to practice two numbers— Mendelssohn's *Capriccio Brilliant* and *Totentanz* (Dance of Death) by Liszt.

On the night of the concert the small figure was almost smothered with flowers as her old admirers from the entire Bay Area crowded the Auditorium to welcome a loved player back to the platform.

"I'd like to have you in Symphony Hall again," Fiedler said as they left the Green Room after all their mutual admirers had gone. "Let me know if you are ever coming east."

Many months passed before that opportunity came. Then, when a cousin was to be married in New York, Ruth wrote. Fiedler must have been on tour, for six weeks passed with no reply. The sensitive pianist thought she had been forgotten until a telegram came from Boston, "Want you on Pops program. Arthur Fiedler."

Her own book "Forbidden Childhood," describes in touching detail her nervous dread of facing the Boston audience as she and her husband walked out of Symphony Hall after the morning rehearsal, but she also shares the generous applause that audience gave her. Fiedler was overjoyed at his re-discovery of her mature talent. Back stage he offered more opportunity. "Would you like to go on tour?" Acceptance of that invitation began a rare friendship.

"Whenever I need an orchestra to go with a record-ing," Ruth said years later, "I turn to Arthur Fiedler. If he needs a pianist, he often asks me to play."

Fiedler was not the only one to take pride in Ruth's renewed career. Across the continent in San Francisco, Alexander Fried mused: "A critic rarely has an oppor-tunity to help in such a special way. Ruth's emergence from virtual retirement from the concert stage had a really miraculous consequence. She not only toured with Fiedler, but came out into the world's public eye per-manently and at least as brilliantly as ever. She has been touring ever since, now on her own as an internationally famous musician. Her records, too, are widely acclaimed."

Not many lives fill with events as spectacular as those which have crowded this artist's years; but the roster of performing guests in the San Francisco Pops series is as full of names familiar to concert-goers every-where as is that of Boston.

One of these young soloists, violinist David Abel, credits the beginning of his major platform career to Arthur Fiedler's discerning ear. David's teacher, Na-houm Blinder, then Concert-master of the San Francisco Symphony, invited the Pops Maestro to his home to listen to this talented pupil in the summer of 1952. Pleasure lit Fiedler eyes as the slight sixteen-year-old drew his bow across the strings with surety that indicated complete identification of player and instrument. As accurate fingers expressed inner warmth and perception Fiedler admitted to himself that Joe Dyer had not been exaggerating when he had quoted Alexander Fried's comment after the lad's first appearance on the program of a San Francisco Symphony Youth Concert two years earlier that he was a "precociously impressive violinist." As David laid down his bow, Fiedler offered him a place on the program he was planning for the following Pops Season.

Thus it was a packed house on an August night in 1953 applauded David Abel's rendition of a Wieniawski *Violin Concerto* with an ovation that one reviewer described as "the noisiest and most spectacular I have witnessed in ten years." Fiedler's immediate invitation brought a repetition of the same performance to Symphony Hall the next spring. From this success, David went on to a triumphant Town Hall debut in New York in October, winning unanimous praise from Manhattan critics and a tour sponsorship by Columbia Artists Management that made his name familiar throughout the United States and Canada. Fiedler listened with pride when Monteux, as guest conductor, included David on a Friday afternoon concert in Symphony Hall. By the time he had Abel on another San Francisco Pops program during the tenth anniversary season in 1960, the gifted soloist produced such tones from his magnificent Guarnerius that *Chronicle* reviewer Dean Wallace said that if Mendelssohn had heard his concerto that night, "he might have cheered himself hoarse!"

Another of the many violinists whose talent was early recognized by Fiedler was Jaime Laredo, character-

ized by "Time" a few years later as the "Prodigious Fiddler." His first teacher, Antonnio Di Grazzi, had also
been a member of the San Francisco Symphony. Di
Grazzi's composition, *La-Re-Do,* was dedicated to the
youth who went on to win the Queen Elizabeth Prize
scholarship in Belgium.

Opera singers who, like Lucine Amara, have San
Francisco backgrounds, have been brought to the Auditorium stage to sing with Arthur Fiedler's Pops. Ray-
mond Manton, tenor of the San Francisco Opera, owes
much to the Director who presented him during the first
season; while the Metropolitan lists Ronald Rietan
among its baritones, and among sopranos stunning black-
haired Florence Quarturaro, a graduate of San Francisco
State College, who delighted a Fiedler audience in 1954,
with her dramatic aria, *La Mamma Morte.*

On one unforgettable August night in 1958 Im-
presario Sol Hurok came back stage after a San Francisco
Pops concert to offer a contract to Grace Bumbry—who
one day would play Lady Macbeth superbly at the Salzburg Festival and star as a member of the Paris Opera.
Satisfaction in the career of this exceptionally talented
young Negro could be shared equally by Fiedler and by
Dyer, who suggested her after he heard her at Lotte Leh-
mann's Music Academy of the West in Santa Barbara
when she won the Southwest Regional Metropolitan Audition of the Air. Also winner of the 1957 Marian Anderson Award, the young mezzo-soprano was acclaimed for

her "lovely appearance and remarkably beautiful voice" after her San Francisco performance.

When Josefa Heifitz came to audition as a pianist, Fiedler told the Art Commission Secretary that he was putting her on the program, not because of her famous father, but because she was such a finished artist in her own right. The list of other eminent pianists whose choice as San Francisco Pops soloist has led to distinguished careers is long. To recall just a few, there are names like Samuel Lipman, who later appeared in Boston in duo with Leo Litwin on The Esplanade and in many a Fiedler concert on both sides of the continent; the former child prodigy, Stephen Bishop; the Greek virtuoso, Dino Ginapoulous, who went from California to success in London.

At the closing concert of the 1957 San Francisco Pops a slender French-descended youth named Ozan Marsh played the Liszt *Piano Concert No. 1* with such eclat that Fiedler invited him at once to tour with him the following season Marsh, who had graduated from Fontainebleau "magna cum laude" as its most outstanding student, had worked with Robert Casadesus and before that with Emil Sauer, one of the last living pupils of Franz Liszt. Marsh's enthusiasm for that composer led him to devote full time to study of the complex works of Liszt. His interpretation of the *Piano Concerto in E-Flat Major,* and later of the works of the Soviet composer, Dimitri Kabalevsky, has contributed distinction to Fied-

ler programs in Boston and across the entire United
States as he traveled again with the touring Pops in 1962.

America is grateful to the discerning conductor
who has, in the words of Marian Anderson, "made such
an unique contribution to music in our country and has
given so many deserving young musicians a chance to be
heard widely." But the unusual event which literally
brought millions into the audience of the photogenic
Bostonian was a performance on Constitution Pier in
Portsmouth, New Hampshire, in June, 1957.

On that summer day the SS *Christian Radich* of
Oslo docked for a sequence of the filming of Louis de
Rochemont's Cinemiracle, *Windjammer*. One of the
student seamen, eighteen-year-old Sven Eric Liebach,
had been practicing the Grieg *Piano Concerto* on all his
off-duty hours crossing the oceans. At the pier ready to
move right into rehearsal was an obviously appropriate
orchestra—the Boston Pops under its impeccably dressed
conductor. Sweat wilted his fresh white shirt as Fiedler
spent the hot morning perfecting the unison of soloist
and accompanying symphony players.

At last a voice over a megaphone shouted: "Dead
quiet on the dock, please! O.K. Roll it!"

The audience, clad in bathing suits, shorts and
dungarees, leaned against railings or perched on coils of
rope, stopped their chatter as the medley of scraping
bows and vibrant woodwinds brought the orchestra into
tune. Then they stood at attention as Arthur Fiedler
stepped briskly to the podium, his white coat shining in

the sun. He raised his baton and the silence was broken by the thunderous crescendo of gleaming kettle drums. The brilliant opening chords of the first movement of the concerto were struck by strong fingers as the composer's young compatriot bent over the keys, squinting behind his horn rimmed glasses. As the glorious melody poured out over the blue water the cinescope recorded picture and sound for posterity.

Before another year passed, Arthur Fiedler was in Oslo for a command performance of the first European showing of *Windjammer* on April 25, 1958. In the audience was King Olaf with his two daughters and his son. As Arthur saw the tall monarch again, his mind leapt back to that special Norwegian Night at The Pops when the then Crown Prince had been his own guest.

The Fiedler-conducted radio concert which highlighted this 1958 visit to the Land of the Mid-Night Sun was full of zest. The unmistakable rhythm which had caused the lady in the remote village to identify a Fiedler record with "America" left friendly echoes in the land of the Norsemen, and Arthur Fiedler flew back to begin another Boston Pops Season.

CHAPTER TEN

Buses and Jets

SIX YEARS BEFORE *Windjammer* made his face familiar on movie screens Arthur Fiedler undertook a musical mission throughout the mid-continent. He had already accepted invitations to guest-conduct symphony orchestras in large cities like Chicago, Montreal, Seattle, and Dallas. But complaints from Boston visitors who found the Pops always "sold out" had convinced him that there were potential audiences from Main Streets everywhere. Just as he had once sensed the music hunger of Boston's multitudes and prepared summer feasts by The Charles, so now he determined to sow the seeds of musical understanding across the wide plains of America.

His own Pops and Esplanade players were committed to the regular series of the Boston Symphony Orchestra; but wherever he traveled as guest conductor his ear was alert for qualified musicians among the many who always came to him for auditions. When he decided in 1952 to organize a Boston Pops Tour Orchestra he knew where to send for players.

167

These men arrived from all over the country for a stiff rehearsal schedule in Symphony Hall. In mid-January Fiedler felt that the ensemble was ready. Off they went on icy roads—two bus loads of musicians and instruments, with the Fiedler Cadillac driven by John Cahill, a non-playing Boston crony of the conductor, in the lead.

There was gay camaraderie among these men. Often as they gathered for lunch or dinner, nostalgic memories of his apprenticeship in touring colored the conductor's conversation. Sometimes he related tales of his youth as a member of the Blüthner Orchestra Tour in Scandinavia, when his father had insisted on early morning practice, no matter how late the previous night's concert had been. Or he would describe the ornate and compact opera house in Helsinki, with high-burning torches marking its entrance off the dark street. He chuckled as he told them of the autocratic miserly Johann Strauss III herding his string ensemble into a dismal Rathskeller in Hamburg.

Recollection of the Sinfonietta tours of the early 'thirties had more local flavor. Then three Fiedlers had gypsied together. Elsa's Berlin-trained fingers had rippled through Chopin waltzes and Liszt cadenzas, and Uncle Benny had kept a watchful eye on his younger relatives. In those days rumbling buses had carried these touring musicians through small communities and college towns along the Atlantic seaboard as far south as Sweet Briar and Randolph-Macon in Virginia.

The story of a side trip into the back country intrigued his new companions. This account came to mind when the Pops Tour men were indulging in a favorite game—"Where were you two nights ago?", with a map spread across their knees. They happened to be in Pennsylvania that evening. Fiedler pointed to a remote spot in the mountains which he said had called for a hundred-mile detour on one of the Sinfonietta tours. Someone had noted the name, "Fiedler," on the earlier map, and the bus driver had been instructed to change course. The Pops maestro laughed as he told his 1953 companions how the three Fiedlers on that trip had planned a surprise concert they would give for unsuspecting "relatives"!

He described late afternoon shadows lengthening across the road as they passed long white barns and wide-verandahed farm houses; but when they came to the town they sought, he said that they had found only two dilapidated houses and an old blacksmith shop. Here the sound of the anvil ceased suddenly and an old man stepped out to watch the tired travelers alighting under a shady sycamore. He pronounced the name "Fiddler" and answered Arthur's questions with tales of pre-Revolutionary ancestors who had settled in these parts long ago. Before the musicians departed on their interrupted tour, Uncle Benny had taken his beloved Guarnerius out of its case and played a solo for the delighted smithy. Arthur Fiedler told his listeners that he could still remember the furrowed face of the old man standing in the twilight

waving a hand reddened over glowing coals, as the bus
rounded a curve and sped on in search of a stopping
place for the night.

There was a twinkle in his brown eyes as the conductor contrasted the audience that had greeted them
when they reached Sweet Briar. There gracious faculty
members and intelligent music-lovers from the college
town had crowded back stage after the concert to admire
all of the rare instruments carried by the ensemble—
Gagliano and Gabrielli violins in addition to Uncle
Benny's Guarnerius. And reminiscent pleasure heightened his description of the southern belles who begged
his autograph.

Now, twenty years later, there was only one Fiedler—their gray-haired and distinguished conductor—as
the 1953 orchestra continued on its mission of sharing his
blend of classical and modern music in sixty-one cities
and twenty-one states. That first year on the road they
gave sixty-four concerts in sixty-eight days—a pace that
continued to accelerate with succeeding annual tours.

Exhilaration of new audiences seems to conquer
fatigue. The Maestro declares that "it is not hard to play
the same things night after night; but rather, a challenge
to meet the needs of each community."

When they returned from the fourth tour—this
time, eighty-one concerts in eighty-three days, with the
area covered extending to the Pacific Coast—Fiedler
summed up the results. "A tour like this makes a lot of

friends for music," he told the welcoming representatives of the Boston press.

That seemed to compensate for windshields broken by whirring rocks, stolen hub caps in Los Angeles, smashed car doors in Seattle. He told his Symphony Hall associates that the applause of small town music-lovers was thanks enough for all the effort, and boasted to Ellen that alert collegiate audiences proved that finally the younger generation of Americans was rivalling Europeans in cultivated musical taste. When RCA-Victor reported increasing record sales, he knew that his young admirers meant what they said when they told him that studying to music helped them retain book knowledge.

Because he has such fatherly interest in youth, he was willing to add one unexpected stint of conducting when the caravan stopped in Manchester, Indiana. Three hundred string players from all of that state's major high schools and collges had traveled over wintry roads for the privilege of working under a noted conductor. When he recounted the experience he told a reporter: "I thought I was in a forest as I looked down on all those bows from a dizzily-high podium. A draft threatened the score every time a page was turned . . . but all that really counted was the stimulated interest in music." Scarcity of good string players is one of Fiedler's constant worries, as he noted the trend among students toward woodwinds, brass, and percussion.

Only one concert was missed. That was on a wintry

night in Rockford, Illinois. The Fiedler car pulled into the parking lot five minutes before curtain time to be informed that State Troopers had halted the buses far back on the icy roads. Insurance covered the refund; but the disappointed audience exacted promise of the same program for the next year.

Another time only the instrument truck was delayed by a blizzard. Fiedler's car and the bus loads of players arrived just as the audience was gathering. Ruth Slenczynska was guest soloist on that tour—one of the four seasons she spent with the Boston Pops Tour Orchestra. The conductor turned to his young friend.

"Ruth, these people must be entertained. Will you please go right on stage and play for them."

The girl had memorized classics since her debut at the age of four walked in, wearing her rumpled travel suit. She sat at the grand piano for an hour, holding the audience enthralled with Beethoven's *Moonlight Sonata* and familiar numbers by Liszt, Chopin, and Mendelssohn, until the truck finally arrived. Instruments were hastily unpacked, players scrambled into dress clothes (also carried in the truck), and the delayed concert proceeded. At the proper place in the program Ruth swept in, wearing her satin formal, to play Rachmaninoff's *Fantasy on a Theme of Paganini*. In spite of all she had played before, the audience was not satisfied until she came back to give them her favorite encore, a Bach Fugue.

Curtain calls are the wine that keeps Fiedler exuberance bubbling. "That was a large, but unenthusiastic audience," he remarked when one conservative group called for only two encores during an entire evening. Usually the cards which the concert-master holds up to announce an encore are well worn by the time the touring group returns to Boston. That is one custom which keeps the atmosphere like the Boston Pops, sans refreshments. Only in San Francisco where the Auditorium is so large that it would be difficult to read the placards, the concert-master uses a microphone. Here, Fiedler sometimes extemporizes—like the time when he asked Henry Schweid to announce—"Now we will play *Pop Goes the Weasel,* by special promise to two very small girls who ought to be home in bed."

Other requests were better ignored—especially the one which interrupted a number when a very flustered waitress made her way to the podium with a note. The conductor took it with his free left hand, and glanced at it. Gallery observers swear the sparks flew from his angry eyes as he dropped the card to the floor and ground it under foot. Joe Dyer got the real repercussion when he opened the door to the dressing room after the concert. There he found the Maestro in a rage—the only time in all their years of close association when he had heard the slightest rise in the affable pitch of Fiedler's voice.

"Throw her out . . . throw her out . . . have her dismissed!" ranted the red-faced conductor, known to Dyer heretofore as a man as methodically courteous as a Boston banker.

The Art Commission Secretary was nonplussed. "What are you talking about? I haven't seen anything wrong!"

"Well, where were you?" Fiedler screamed. "You couldn't have missed that clod-hopping imbecile, weaving in and out between the violins." Fiedler clomped around the little room, imitating the clumsy girl. "I supposed she was bringing a note from you, saying, 'Stop the music—the Russians are attacking'!"

It took Dyer almost ten minutes to calm his angry friend sufficiently to find out what had happened while he had been tied up in the box office. Then he learned that some over-exuberant champagne drinker had evidently tipped the waitress well to carry the man's card to the podium. "Please play *Happy Birthday* to my wife" was all it said. In the end Dyer and Fiedler had a good laugh, and Dyer opened the door to the usual impatient horde of autograph seekers.

Fans would sometimes recognize Fiedler in strange places. Philip Clark tells of an evening in Portland, Oregon, when he and Arthur were enjoying a quiet supper in a small restaurant after a Boston Pops Tour concert. A burly man in a booth across from them eyed the Maestro menacingly. Finally, as they were about to leave the man rose to his full six feet-four and squared his bulging shoulders as he faced Fiedler.

"You cost me a thousand dollars tonight," he blurted, glowering down at the dapper conductor. "You took my audience away from the prize fight—but," he added, pulling a folded program from his pocket, "I'll forgive you, if you will autograph this for my wife. She made me promise to follow you until I got it!"

Samplings of reviews heaped in boxes on Fiedler shelves reveal the whole gamut of response to the touring Pops. One Ohio critic wrote: "We of the great middle section of the country who must content ourselves with musical 'crusts' wonder if the people of Boston appreciate having a group like this for their own." (The writer evidently did not know that this was not the real Boston Pops, and that those of the mid-continent only had such music because of the initiative of the conductor who built up this touring organization for the very purpose that prompted the praise.)

Claudia Cassidy of the "Chicago Tribune" did not agree with the Ohio Writer. Many inches of her column continually debunked the popular appeal of the Pops conductor as she asserted that: "I can't stand Fiedler." A Detroit critic considered the touring musician "valid, but not vivacious, despite the energetic angular motions of the conductor." In contrast, a Florida commentator described Fiedler as "a gracious, relaxed self-effacing conductor, who evidently leaves the tensions in the rehearsals where they belong, offering a smoothly functioning ensemble for the concert."

If that writer had been sitting among the players during a rehearsal he would have discovered that the "smooth functioning" was achieved through good humor rather than temper. The Fiedler assumption that all are working together toward a common goal—the pleasure of the audience—is usually the best incentive to good performance. But restlessness can bring a plea, "Come on now"—most often prefaced with a "please."—"Don't talk so much. . . . I'm working hard. Cooperate, it's your show." Many a time a laugh draws the players together in a difficult place when Fiedler's language becomes picturesque. "Make it sound like molasses," he told The Cecilia Chorus struggling to get a smooth ensemble. A "grace note is like a preposition, not a proposition," he tells a violist. "Hold the reins in check," he suggested to the violins in Enesco Gypsy music as he posed like the driver of wild horses. "I've played with Georges Enesco. Make it light."

Innate rhythm and sure pitch always lead to detection of the slightest variance in any instrument. When the percussionist's whistle did not sound like the station master's signal in Strauss' *Exposition Train,* Fiedler amused the whole group with his own demonstration—placing two fingers in his mouth and producing the sound exactly in tune. In the meantime Joe Sinai was digging frantically in his bag for a better whistle.

He can make clipped staccato directions sound like almost any brass or woodwind, and his baton becomes an imaginary bow as he explains the way to hold it to get a desired effect. "Sing!" He turns to the violas—"Use an up bow. . . . make it like silk"; or, pointing to the player's wrist, "use a little oil in there."

Koussevitzky's successor in Boston, Charles Munch, described what many players have come to feel in their relation to Fiedler when he explained in his book, "I Am a Conductor," what he considered the optimum conductor-player relationship. Munch wrote that it is not a problem of command, but one of communication. Here the medium is not speech, but gesture and the influence the conductor radiates.

Players feel this radiation from Fiedler. They are willing to acept any amount of needed correction. He plays no favorites. If it is Dickson in Boston, or Joe Sinai in San Francisco, he stops the rehearsal and tells the man in question just what seems wrong to him. Sometimes the percussion section thinks they bear the brunt. He is known as the toughest critic of this particular group, for in his study of the score he pays as much attention to the most minute tinkle of a triangle as to the melodic line in the strings. But whatever he says in rehearsal is forgotten as soon as the mistake is corrected. San Francisco's lone woman percussionist, Peggy Cunningham Lucchesi, remembers well a morning when she seemed the butt of all the conductors' ire, as he ripped violently into her rhythm. Lunch hour came. The group filed out to Fiedler's favorite small Viennese restaurant around the corner on Grove Street.

"Well, how are we going to sit?" asked Fiedler. "Come on, Peggy, let's start over here," and he led her to the corner booth.

Whether conducting the Boston Pops, the Touring

Pops, or the San Francisco Pops, Fiedler collected personnel sheets. If a horn player had been on leave for a season or two, he would welcome him back the next time his name appeared on the printed list. "How's the contracting business?" asked the conductor as they gathered in the tuning room.

He talks with his men and learns about their families, their plans for children's musical education, their vacation travels; and he keeps a careful record of all his regular players so that he can divide the employment of every one of them fairly between outside jobs on radio, TV and special events.

He even had a personal barber in his Tour Orchestra. Because of his habit of talking music wherever he goes, he found a young tuba player in a barber shop in Providence, Rhode Island. Dante DiNunzio closed shop for two months each winter, so that he could share the experience of touring with the man who schools himself and all around him to strive for perfection in every performance.

In spite of the fact that they perform the same program over and over for different audiences, Fiedler would hunt a piano at every stop, taking time to play over parts of the orchestration "to understand better what happens." Then he would turn to his group with the admonition to "play each piece as if it were the first time this audience has ever heard it." Every player in the Tour Orchestra was urged to practice "in order to feel secure," while the ensemble was polished through frequent rehearsals to improve the total effect.

Regardless of this, the Tours were not all work. Arthur Fiedler relished the social sidelights with the zest of his early Boston days. His gourmet food tastes are constantly publicized; but one hostess failed to pay attention. The house where she staged an after-concert reception was elegant and drinks were plentiful. But the slight refreshments left Arthur unsatisfied. The evening wore on. In desperation, her honor guest asked for a tour of the home, including the kitchen.

"What a splendid refrigerator," he remarked. "I'll bet it's full of good things."

She opened the gleaming door, revealing two small broilers on the first shelf. "I'm sure you are an expert cook," teased Fiedler.

"Just let me demonstrate," she replied, taking out the chickens. "Show me how you like them."

That evening ended well, with the conductor sitting contentedly in the kitchen, stripping meat off the almost burned chicken, cooked without any butter as per his instructions.

A Milwaukee experience was in sharp contrast. His hosts, the Karl Ratzsdkes, Jr. and Sr., set out to prove that anything he had eaten elsewhere on his journeys could be prepared and served in their restaurant as well or better than anywhere else. He was invited to a gala affair, honoring both Fiedler and the chairman of the

Pops ticket sales. Iranian caviar served in a dish on tinted ice sculptured into the shape of a violin was accompanied by vodka. Then came Burgundy and oysters, curried puree of chuker partridge on Indienne noodles, Strasbourg goose, flown from France, roasted and stuffed with wild rice and truffles, and served with Bavarian red cabbage. Dessert was flaming Cherries Jubilee over ice cream resting in half pineapples. Arthur Fiedler was not hungry that night!

That city offered more than a banquet. Among the enthusiastic young people in the Milwaukee Auditorium on the night of the Pops Concert there was a young man who followed the conductor to Chicago to seek an audition. Fiedler listened to Ralph Votapek on an old piano in the restaurant of the Blackstone Hotel. An invitation to solo at the Boston Pops that season was instantaneous —a story proudly remembered by Fiedler's Symphony Hall associates when the Wisconsin youth won the 1962 Van Cliburn Award four years later. Here was another of those musical "foster sons," whose success added to Fiedler's reputation as "one of the country's best talent scouts."

Such a rating was won through many years of farsighted selection of guest artists considered worthy of return invitations. One of these was the Spanish-American pianist, Agustin Anievas, who won the first prize in the original Mitropolous Competition, as well as the Michaelis Award. These are but two of the many faces that come into focus when Fiedler recounts the long list of performers neatly pigeonholed in his mind. He probably knows the musicians of the Americas more personally than any other conductor. But it is not likely that he can recall the individual identities of one of the first group of players he met in the capacity of guest conductor.

He likes to tell of the ragged band of barefoot Indians in Uxmal, whose leader offered him the baton for a concert among the Mayan ruins during a Central American vacation in 1936. His host, an M.I.T. engineer working in Yucatan, had become friendly with these native musicians. He introduced the visiting Maestro. The men had no scores. Their instruments were strange to Fiedler. Yet someway, without a spoken word, the international language of music brought rapport. He picked up the crude baton, and to his surprise, found them ready to play Beethoven's *Egmont Overture* and the *Hungarian Dances* of Brahms among the other pieces that rang out in that hot dusty air.

His next appearance in Latin America came twenty-one years later. The great Argentinian National Radio Orchestra was larger than the Boston Symphony Orchestra. One-hundred and ten men, many of them second-generation Italian, German and Austrian musicians, looked up to follow his beat as Fiedler stepped to the improvised podium in the assembly room of the University of Law. A strike had closed the magnificent Teatro Colon where the concerts had been scheduled; but the music these descendants of pioneer South American immigrants produced under the *simpatico* conductor from North America brought thousands to the substitute auditorium. For his part, he was thoroughly enjoying the exceptional players, pleased that their cultural inheritance meant that he could converse with most of them in the languages of their fathers.

It was not long before the musical rhythms of the Spanish language, too, grooved into his brain. Under careful tutelage from local RCA-Victor representatives he answered radio interviewers, and smilingly acknowledged seekers in record shops in smooth Spanish phrases.

Adjustment to the timing of South American hospitality and concert schedules was more difficult. His life-time rule of morning rehearsals, a main noon-time meal, and a rest before the concert was rudely revised. Rehearsals here lasted from two-thirty to five-thirty in the afternoon. What his hosts called Matinee or *Vermouth* concerts began at nine-thirty and lasted till mid-night. A morning "constitutional" near the Alvear Palace became a necessity to keep the popular conductor fit.

Nine concerts in the twenty days he spent in beautiful cosmopolitan Buenos Aires were indeed a prelude to the words inscribed two years later on that gold plaque presented on The Esplanade to "one of the world's outstanding ambassadors of good music."

Before he left The Argentine after the first visit in 1957, his many new friends entertained him at a large reception. After the other guests left, he lingered to fraternize with the exciting floor show performers. Their native drum, made from a hollowed-out section of a tree-trunk covered at each end by stretched goat skin, intrigued this collector of strange instruments. He was now in the company of cultured musicians, not the superstitious Haitian voodoo drummers he had unsuspectedly offended twenty years before. The Arballo brothers were gracious instructors, highly impressed by the Boston conductor's quick mastery of their *Bom-bo*. Once he caught that rhythm, he wanted to learn the guacho dance step that went with their folk song, *Zapeto*. Dawn was breaking in the Southern Hemisphere autumn sky when Fiedler walked out of the great hall, resplendent in the flaming red poncho his new friends had draped around his shoulders.

With this bright tribute hung over his arm and *Hasta la vista, simpatico Maestro* ringing in his ears, Arthur Fiedler boarded a northbound plane—promising to repeat the visit a year later.

Ellen and the Philip Clarks were with him when he took off from New York on an Argentine Airline flight in April, 1958. At midnight they stopped to re-fuel in Trinidad. Music from a fifteen-piece steel band floated on the velvet-soft night air; but not as a welcome for the traveling Bostonians. It was just the usual pastime of the one night club in the Colony, located at the airport.

In Buenos Aires there was a difference. Argentinians had not forgotten their *simpatico* friend. Clark snapped many a picture of "A.F." standing below his own smiling visage as huge posters saying *Welcome,*

Maestro Fiedler, greeted them on stucco walls wherever they turned.

This year he conducted the Colon Opera Orchestra in Centennial Park where Jacaranda trees shown in full moonlight to form a lacy backdrop, and the footlights raised a screen of buzzing mosquitoes. Crouched between these trees, their appealing eyes glistening in the lights, two soft-coated llamas listened with the aplomb of sophisticated symphony enthusiasts.

By now his Argentinian friends had discovered the Fiedler preference for morning rehearsals. The schedule was more to his liking. He found time to roam among their music shops, picking up unusual scores. One, a ballet suite from *Estancia* by Alberto Ginastera, went into his briefcase to be presented at the Boston Pops. At the same time that he was enjoying exposure to Latin-American music he was introducing representative North American compositions, like *Rhapsody in Blue*—played by Wilenski, a distinguished Argentinian pianist—for the first time in South America.

Two years later he abandoned his usual Boston Pops Tour Orchestra to accept another return engagement in The Argentine. On a blustery morning early in February the Pops conductor was boarding a jet at Logan Airport, his briefcase bulging with music scores and his spirit dedicated to an unofficial but earnest Inter-American Goodwill mission. This time his three concerts in Buenos Aires were to be special in character. The first one, all Viennese, would honor the country of

his own ancestors and that of many of the second-generation Austrians he now included among his close musical
friends in that great Argentinian orchestra. Next, he
planned an evening of all-ballet music; but the third
concert was really geared to his mission. That was to be
All-American, featuring Gottschalk, Copland, Gershwin,
Bernstein, Gould, Guarniera (*Dansa Brasileira*), and
Ginastera's *Two Dances from Ballet Estancia.*

When he reached Buenos Aires Fiedler found
unexpected allies. The United States Navy Band had
landed in the southern port. As he joined the throng
gathered to listened to the blue-jackets in the public
square, he was recognized by their conductor, Commander Charles Brendler.

"Arthur Fiedler!" exclaimed the officer with beam-
ing pleasure, "Please, Sir, will you take the stick?", and
he pressed the shining baton into the hand of the astonished Bostonian. *The Stars and Stripes Forever* echoed
along the shore with all the fervor Sousa had intended
as the symphony conductor made his unofficial debut as
a bandmaster.

A new outlet for Fiedler energy opened with that
chance performance. When he returned to Boston an
invitation lay on his desk from Lee W. Peterson, Execu-
tive Secretary of the All-American Bandmaster's Band.
Commander Brendler had been so impressed by the
Buenos Aires performance that he had suggested that
Fiedler be asked to conduct the Mid-West National Band
Clinic in Chicago in December of that year. The letter

told him that his would be the largest band convention in the world, to meet in its fourteenth consecutive gathering "to provide leadership and further opportunities for directors to gain inspiration and information for an advanced school program . . . we would not only like you to conduct the band of one-hundred of the finest school music directors recruited from the United States and Canada—all professionals—but we would also be honored to have you as guest speaker at our banquet. You may speak for fifteen minutes on a subject of your choice."

"Will you do *that?*" Fiedler's secretary asked with some apprehension, knowing so well his aversion to public speaking.

"Why not?" he replied unhesitatingly. "It might be fun."

But other pleasures filled the months before acceptance of that invitation took him to Chicago. When his Argentinian engagement was completed, he flew over the Andes to conduct the *Orcuesta Filarmonica de Chile* in Santiago. Here the papers praised Arthur Fiedler, *Impulsivo y flamatico a las vez.* Gay hours were spent with *dos affectionados* in out door cafés along the boulevards of the seaside resort of Vina del Mar. Breezes from the sapphire Pacific wafted stirring music over attentive crowds gathered to listen to concerts in the open.

The Pops conductor was in Rio, too, before that year ended—with a flight to Brazil in September. The flavorful coastal shrimp delighted gourmet-Fiedler. Then when he stepped onto the podium of the magnificent theatre to signal his players for the opening note of his first concert before a Brazillian audience his pulse beat fast; he was on the very spot where Toscanini stood when he made his conducting debut! The presence of the famed Hungarian pianist, Lili Krauss, as guest soloist, added to his pleasure in this tour. He left the country gratified by the reviews which designated him as a popular *regente de musica erudite de mondo*.

Jets took the Fiedlers in a new direction the following year. Early in March they were on an El Al plane bound for Israel. Another man beloved in Boston, poet Robert Frost, traveled with them. The two New Englanders were to be among the honorees at the gala opening of the Sheraton-Tel Aviv. Six years before, Frost and Fiedler had stood together to receive homage from fellow citizens in the Boston Public Gardens. Now they were going half-way around the world to be a part of a Twenty-fifth Aniversary of a unique cultural institution —the Israeli Philharmonic, which Arthur would lead in two concerts.

Emotion surged in Fiedler hearts as the bare hills of Palestine spread below the circling jet coming in to land at Lydda Airport. Ellen's fingers involuntarily made a sign of the Cross as she looked for the first time on The Holy Land. Arthur's mind leapt with anticipation as he thought of standing before the aggregation of musicians whose zeal for music had paralleled driving desire for a country. He had met and talked with some of these men and women the year before, when world-touring Israelis had stirred a Symphony Hall audience under the baton of Josef Krips. Fiedler recalled the eletrifying effect of their rendition of Honegger's dark and troubled Second Symphony, created out of the Nazi occupation of France.

On the morrow he—Arthur Fiedler—would stand before these musicians, many of whom had played under Toscanini a quarter of a century before in their first concert on December 26, 1936. He remembered, too, the pride with which Koussevitzky had brought the then Palestine Symphony to Boston on their first United States tour in 1950. Koussevitzky, and Munch after him, had both put their hearts into the success of this orchestra, which had often called them across the world to conduct.

Fiedler sensed that in a way his presence in Israel was the direct result of a service he had rendered the dying Koussevitzky. Some years before the Russian Maestro, who in so many ways had thwarted the ambitions of his Boston colleague, had called him to his bedside.

"Artur," he had said, "I cannot fulfill my obligation to conduct the American Fund for Israel concert at Ebbetts Field next week. You must do it for me. Soloists are to be Jan Peerce, Piatigorsky, and Regina Resnik."

This was in the middle of a Pops season. Fiedler took his problem to George Judd. "What *can* I do?" he asked the wise manager.

"This is a command performance," Judd declared. "Get a guest conductor for the Pops. You must do this."

That concert had brought Arthur Fiedler tremendous appreciation from influential supporters of Israel at home and overseas. Several invitations to lead the Tel Aviv Orchestra had followed; but never before had his schedule allowed acceptance. Now at last his name would be placed on the list of famous conductors who had contributed to the world-wide reputation of this unique ensemble of artist-refugees from many lands. That list included, in addition to Toscanini, the von Weingartners—Felix and his wife Carmen—Molinari, Mitropoulos, Ormandy, Iturbi, Leinsdorf, Bernstein, and numerous others.

Yet it was not the Philharmonic which first responded to the Fiedler baton in Tel Aviv. He was standing in the ornate lobby of the new Sheraton on opening day when the Tel Aviv Police Band marched in. Their band master quickly recognized the man newly dubbed "Band Master of Band Masters" and proferred his baton. As readily as he had led the United States Navy Band in the Buenos Aires Plaza, Fiedler took the stick; he directed the uniformed Israelis with all the gusto he pours into a Sousa march with the Boston Police Band on opening day of the Red Sox season!

The friendliness of that introduction reflected in the applause that greeted the democratic conductor after he had donned formal attire to lead the two scheduled concerts. One of these was given in the hotel ballroom;

the other, in the four-year-old Mann Auditorium with its three-thousand seats all filled. Not only did he include classic numbers by Tchaikowsky, Rossini, Debussy and Offenbach, but he also spiced the evenings with characteristic music of the Americas—the *Porgy and Bess Suite,* reminiscent of his early Gershwin friendship, and Ginastera numbers brought from his recent South American tours.

Five days in Israel were all all too short; but that is the way Arthur Fiedler lives. He was due in Boston for numerous commitments, including rehearsals for a new musical venture.

The previous summer after an Esplanade concert the head of the Boston Opera Group had been chatting casually with a number of friends as Fiedler stepped out of his Shell dressing room. She started to congratulate him on the evening's program.

"You know," he said, half-jestingly interrupting her, "I've always wanted to try my hand at opera. How about next season?"

"Splendid!" explained Miss Caldwell. "You're just the man we're looking for. We're thinking of putting on *Die Fledermaus* in the spring."

"Fun!" Fiedler's eyes shapped in anticipation. He accepted on the spot, with no thought of what the calendar might hold next April. "My father once held a post in a small opera company in Berlin. He enjoyed it. You can count on me."

Fun it proved, even to the marquee signs which blazoned:

DER FIEDLERMAUS
conducted by
ARTHUR FLEDER

on the Donnelly Theatre a block down Massachusetts Avenue from Symphony Hall.

Reviews were headlined *Pop Goes Fledermaus.* Critics commented on the enthusiastic swing his old friends of the Boston Waltz Group had put into the second act of Fiedler-conducted Strauss. One of them, Barbara Walker, was distressed when a writer reported that her sparkling Viennese fan had "outshown the conductor"—as she had obeyed Fiedler's instructions to all "supers" to "keep busy." She apologized to her friend. A quizzical half-smile wrinkled his trim mustache. "Oh hell," he said, "I didn't even notice!"

With this operatic interlude, and the thirty-second season of The Pops behind him, Fiedler was soon back on the jets again. He had tarried in Boston just long enough to open The Esplanade series, now regularly conducted by Dickson. Then San Francisco welcomed him royally with the Municipal Band playing in Union Square in tribute to the eleventh anniversary of the Western Pops.

"We hope," said the President of the Musicians'

Union, whose services had been donated for the occasion, "that Mr. Fiedler keeps coming back like a song and goes on like 'Old Man River.'"

He was still shaking confetti out of his coat pockets when he returned to Boston after the gala farewell concert of that season to prepare for a more serious engagement in England. The confetti shower had been inaugurated a few years before by that perennial left-front balcony seat holder on each closing night. This year she had gone to the Green Room the week before the series was to end to say good-bye before departing on a trip.

"What, no confetti!" There was mock disappointment in Fiedler's voice as he shook her hand.

"Oh, yes, my friends will take care of that," she assured him. But this year the Art Commission, too, had caught the fiesta spirit. Not only confetti from the balcony had showered on the conductor, but the whole orchestra had been tangled in a web of serpentine provided by ushers and waitresses.

When Fiedler arrived in Hastings—the English seacoast town made famous by William the Conqueror—to participiate in their annual Music Festival, the London Philharmonic was waiting for his baton. Here, where the Norman Conquest had changed the course of history, British music-lovers had joined summer visitors for their first face-to-face acquaintance with the American conductor whose recordings made him seem like an old friend. Fiedler's voice, too, was familiar to some of the audience, who remembered the time Sir John Barbirolli had invited the Pops conductor to make the opening address—by transcription—for the Halle Orchestra of Manchester a few years earlier.

Now in the busy summer of 1961 he could not linger more than five days in Britain. New demands called him back to Boston, where "The Globe" was sponsoring a TV series to be known as *The World of Arthur Fiedler*. Some of these programs on WBZ-TV— with fifty-five members of the Boston Pops Orchestra— were to be video-taped for future release later in the autumn when he would again be out of the country. While this was the first series of the kind planned exclusively for Fiedler, it was not his TV debut. *Great Music from Chicago* over Station WGN in the 1959-1960 season had first presented him—along with Monteux, Kostelanetz, Fritz Reiner, Steinberg, and many famous artists. This Chicago series was continuing, and he had to be in the Windy City, as well as in Boston, for studio taping during the three weeks before he and Ellen were again zooming across the Atlantic to meet their British commitments.

It was the BBC Philharmonia which waited his signal this time to open a radio show. At the first long drum roll the studio audience rose, thinking that the Queen was arriving. But the orchestra swept on into the stirring music. People slid back into their seats sheepishly, realizing that the drums had merely played the introduction.

The main purpose of this trip to England was to conduct a concert in the dramatic egg-shaped hall built for the 1951 Festival of Britain on the bank of The Thames. This was Fiedler's first public appearance in London. Applause rang from the cantilevered boxes and protruding galleries as the audience recognized the handsome conductor, who had already been featured on BBC-TV before this concluding performance of his British visit.

Someway, between all these engagements, the two Fiedlers managed a rare bit of holiday together—a few plays, dinners in inconspicuous little restaurants like the Italian *L'Esperance* in Knightsbridge, and a stroll or two among the chrysanthemums and dahlias of Kew Gardens. But Debbie was to celebrate her fourteenth birthday on October 22nd. Her father was due in Dublin that very day. Grudgingly, he gave in to his daughter's claim on her mother. He put Ellen on a home-bound jet before he took a smaller plane to Ireland—with nostalgic longing for his wife's companionship.

Seven years earlier they had had one of their unaccustomed purely vacation trips together to that country. Without a single musical engagement that time, he had managed to tour unrecognized in a "drive-yourself" car rented from Cyril MacCormack, son of the famous singer, who had been a friend of Dr. Bottomley. A French beret concealed the familiar Fiedler hair as Arthur drove along country roads, stopping at sod-thatched cottages in their search for ancestral Bottomley memorabilia. Only in Dublin had they broken the incognito rule to call at the apartment of their Boston friend, Blanche Walker, then living briefly in Ireland. She took them to a unique small restaurant where the proprietor, Michael O'Dwyer, did all the cooking—to the extreme pleasure of gourmet-Fiedler.

When dinner was over, O'Dwyer sat down at the piano and sang old Irish songs in a rich baritone. The night wore on while these congenial musicians lingered over Irish coffee in reminiscent exchange of anecdote and song. Everytime he thinks of Dublin Arthur remembers the gleam in Ellen's eyes when O'Dwyer sang airs from *Brigadoon,* and told them about his courting days in Johannesburg where he and his wife were both members of the cast of that Scottish operetta.

Now, in 1961, Ellen was soaring above the Atlantic as Arthur went on alone to conduct three concerts on *Radio Eireann* in this city they had once enjoyed together. A week later he arrived back at Logan Airport with the harvest moon rising over Boston. At eight o'clock the next morning he and Ellen were on a west-bound jet again, heading for Tokyo and a three-week tour with the Tokyo Symphony throughout the islands where recordings made the Fiedler name and rhythm familiar everywhere.

Japanese concert-goers applauded "the ardent champion disseminating music as a universal language of friendship and understanding." The Tokyo Fire Department was equally hospitable. His ride through the

crowded streets of the world's largest city was more
hazardous than the most exciting fire truck excursions of
his younger Boston years. He brought home colorful in-
signia denoting his rank as Honorary Fire Chief of Japan
to add fantastic decoration to the Brookline entrance
hall.

The Fiedlers left Japan on Thanksgiving Day, too
tired to enjoy their turkey on the plane. Despite exhaus-
tion and Ellen's deep bronchial cold, they both came
back to innumerable duties in holiday-decorated Boston.
After a short weekend with his eager family, Arthur departed to keep guest-conducting engagements in Buffalo
and Philadephia; while Ellen forced herself to bring out
the Christmas ornaments and help the children put up a
tree their father had scarce time to notice.

He was in Boston briefly on his sixty-seventh birthday on December 17th—primarily for the noon-time
taping of *The World of Arthur Fiedler,* released on TV
that night. But when the engineers disconnected their
cables and the Kleig lights went out, players did not put
their instruments back into cases and dash in all directions as they usually did at the end of one of these
sessions. Instead, the concert master picked up Fiedler's
baton. *Happy Birthday to You* resounded through the
Sheraton-Plaza ballroom. Waiters appeared with heaping
trays, tables were wheeled in and the entire orchestra sat
down to honor their leader with a true "surprise party."

Perhaps the lingering pleasure of that noon-hour

helped to compensate for the Chicago engagement that took him to Illinois on Christmas Eve. In early January he flew to British Columbia and was back in Montreal on the tenth. Before he started the seventh of his Boston Pops Tours, he was guest-conducting in Portland, Maine, in early February.

An editorial in the "Portland Evening Express"—captioned *Thank you, Mr. Fiedler*—augured well for the approaching strenuous nine weeks on the road. The winter morning was stormy as he sat among his bags in the Hyslop Road hall. For the first time in his career of ceaseless going, he confessed to Ellen, "I wish I could stay right here!" Then the mailman left an envelope from the clipping bureau. Ellen slit it open casually. Their eyes fell on the words of the Maine journalist.

"In all the broad entertainment firmament," they read, "we know of no single contemporary who had brought us more distinguished or lasting enjoyment. We are grateful for many hours of listening pleasure, which, thanks to scores of records, he will continue to afford. Mr. Fiedler has helped us and many others to become musically respectable by proving that Beethoven and Berlin, Mozart and Mancini are really compatible. He has shown the world respect for popular music. One can enjoy jazz without being a nut. He has brought to thousands the knowledge that they can enjoy classics once believed dull and beyond them."

Ellen's concern vanished as she watched the old

enthusiasm light up the weary face of her husband. "Tuck this in your pocket as a good omen," she said, folding up the clipping.

Bill Schissler came in to pick up the bags and they stepped into the waiting Cadillac to head for Kingston, New York, and whatever musical converts might be gathered there for the opening night of the new tour. Deep in his heart he knew that those 75,000 miles he had covered in whirring around the world during the year just passed had been well spent!

CHAPTER ELEVEN

"Thank Yous" and a Bridge

GRATITUDE FOR ARTHUR FIEDLER's contribution to musical understanding had taken many forms long before those buses and jets brought him face to face with world-wide audiences. Tufts College in Boston had been the first to recognize that he was an educator as well as an entertainer. During the first year after his appointment to the conductorship of The Pops, President John A. Cousens had hung the bright hood signifying an Honorary Master's degree on the shoulders of the young man whose formal academic years had ended with the Boston Latin School.

"This will be a matter of gratification, not only to members of the college community, but to all who have known of your accomplishments," Cousens said as he shook Fiedler's hand.

Soon after the conductor was instructing in his chosen field at the new Malkin Conservatory established by a Boston Symphony 'cellist. Among his colleagues on the faculty was Arnold Schönberg, who was introducing his conception of the use of twelve-tone form to students of composition.

Members of Fiedler's classes were grateful for their teacher's witty comments on the works of this leading exponent of unorthodox musical expression; but he did not impose such experiments on his increasing Esplanade audiences. Those people still needed musical education in works within their comprehension. In appreciation of those concerts for the masses members of the Greek Traditional Society presented a golden laurel wreath—a signal honor heretofore bestowed only on Marathoners.

Other deorations came as The Pops celebrated its Golden Jubilee in 1935. Fiedler's interest in and sympathetic interpretation of French music brought him recognition from the Third Republic as an *Officier de l'Instruction Publique*. In Boston, "The Jewish Advocate," whose columns continually praised his versatile contributions to local culture, bestowed their Carnation—a community badge of approval for good deeds of service. Given weekly to recipients in every walk of life, race or religion, the Carnation has become the oldest continuing award of its kind in the country.

Other eyes were watching appraisingly as Fiedler interests widened. The Cecilia was not the only chorus to reach almost professional status under his meticulous leadership. He made weekly trips to Providence to direct the University Glee Club; and the MacDowell Society Orchestra of Boston looked to him for guidance. In this group of amateurs who played together solely for the pure love of music there was a new member who had joined specifically to observe Fiedler's technique with non-professionals. Albert Sherman, Business Manager of Boston University, had been frankly skeptical when the conductor's name had been mentioned as a possible succesor to Jacques Hoffman, longtime instructor of violin and ensemble at the University.

Soon Sherman's skepticism turned to admiration. He found himself responding to the baton of a man who combined musical scholarship with exceptional insight into the capabilities of these business men and women, who willingly put in grinding hours of practice to perfect their occasional concerts. This director could do great things for the students of Boston University. He reported unreservedly in Fieldler's favor to the Board of Trustees.

Once Fiedler accepted the university post, music critics began to use their complimentary tickets to campus orchestral concerts, intrigued by the number of "firsts" presented here by the daring conductor. Ambitious students, bored with compulsory Haydn and Mozart, flocked to enroll in Fiedler's classes as he challenged their ability to understand Vaughn Williams and Hindemith. A performance of the latter's *Trauermusik,* written the day after King George VI died, and broadcast over BBC, demonstrated the conductor's alertness to current events. When his students presented *Mechanized Forces* by Alexander Luszto, tanks seemed to rumble across the stage as drums rattled and tubas blasted.

In contrast to the modern, he brought out a Bach suite (Overture) in C Major, which had never been heard in Boston. Again, in the more modern mood his orchestra performed Vaughn Williams' *Flos Campi* for the first time in America. When one of his students, Robert D. King, wrote an overture which seemed worthy of presentation, Fiedler premiered it two weeks after he had given a first American performance of *Turkemenia,* a composition by Boris Schechter, a graduate of Odessa Conservatory.

When Fiedler commenced his twenty-first season with The Pops, he was rewarded for all that he had put into his University position. An extraordinary announcement at Boston University Night at The Pops informed the audience that at the June Commencement the conductor would become Dr. Fiedler, with the conferring of an honorary PhD on "one of the Hub City's favorite sons, who has held this post longer than any conductor heading an American Symphony." In commenting on this honor, the "New York Times" remarked that "Fiedler's history and that of the organization he serves have almost become one," adding that, "he will be guest conductor for the New York Philharmonic on June 15 at their *Music Under the Stars* at Ebbets Field."

Celebrations galore heralded the approach of his twenty-fifth anniversary as Pops Conductor four years later. "Nearing sixty," wrote one admirer, "he looks as dapper and zestful as a boulevardier . . . he seems to find fresh enthusiasm for each new season and he conducts each concert, not only with professional smoothness, but with the gusto of a man who likes what he is doing."

That is Arthur Fiedler's secret. He not only likes what he is doing, but he puts tireless effort into sharing that enjoyment. By the time of this anniversary, the red leather books in his Symphony Hall office revealed that he had conducted more than 1,250 Pops concerts in Boston, playing at least a thousand different compositions. If the emphasis had been on light music, it had always been interspersed with enough classics to build audience interest in the regular winter series.

Through the years, Fiedler's partnership in the Boston Symphony contributed immeasurably to the overall success of the whole organization. Because The Pops and The Esplanade provide music for the community and employment for the players during nine of the forty-seven week playing season, Fiedler's part in the accomplishments of this famous orchestra has been marked. While every large symphony organization must depend on extra gifts to meet financial needs, the Boston Symphony earns more of its annual budget than any other orchestra in the United States—more than seventy percent, versus a national average of fifty-seven percent. Box office receipts from the gay spring Pops add encouraging figures in the annual reports.

Fiedler's programming for those weeks for which he is responsible reflects the choices of listeners who request a wide variety of works for all those special nights sponsored by organizations ranging from Harvard University to the Hoo-Hoo Club and the Workmen's Circle. He gives them what they ask for, but he also weaves in rare items from old-time composers—Frescobaldi, Telemann, Bach, Beethoven—along with contemporaries like Prokofieff, Shostakovitch, Poulenc, Piston, and Gershwin.

"There is bad music and good music in all forms," he observes, "What is wrong with the *William Tell Overture?* It is a fine piece, but how often is it heard in the winter series?"

Public thanks to the man who had amalgamated so many forms of musical taste during his twenty-five years on the spring podium of Symphony Hall reached a climax with the Pops' birthday party on May 5, 1954. This was a gay affair. "Yummy" and "Debbie" stood on top of the piano to blow out the twenty-five candles on a huge cake. George Judd, retiring as Manager of the Boston Symphony Orhcestra, complimented the press for the prophetic statement of 1930 that "the Golden Age of The Pops has arrived." Speaking as one who knew the whole story, he assured the audience that those who had predicted "a new era of prosperity" because "under Fiedler The Pops will enjoy a greater vogue than ever" had spoken correctly.

Two musical surprises lent color to the program. When the encore card announced *T Viana,* audience laughter shook the historic hall as the orchestra played quite seriously Hayman's *potpourri* of video singing commercials. In another number percussionist Harold Faberman stepped over into the wood-wind section and blew a duck whistle to change the mood of a conventional arrangement of the popular tune, *Ebb Tide*. Listeners were convulsed by realistic imitations of ducks and other sea life woven into Peter Bodge's musical satire, *Low Tide*.

In contrast to these mirth-provoking numbers, the usual light-hearted closing third of the program also included Jack Mason's arrangement of tunes from *Kismet*, winning elaborate praise from reviewers. "The orchestra was dazzling," said the "Christian Science Monitor," "and played with that panoramic tonal splendor with which Arthur Fiedler leaves his listeners gasping for breath . . . as an encore they played a winsome little piece, *Candlelight Waltz*, also composed by Mason."

Adaptations of Broadway musicals, like this one from *Kismet* commanded Fiedler's most thoughtful attention. They are as important to him as any symphonic work; and he cooperates with the arranger to orchestrate tunes he selects personally in combinations intended to use to the fullest advantage the special abilities of his versatile Pops players. These custom-made arrangements are practically never printed, but are the property of The Pops organization. Each one costs over one thousand dollars—at six dollars a measure; and this does not include the copying charges.

Fiedler found unsuspecting approval from Pierre Monteux for his creative orchestrations of familiar tunes. He was driving the Maestro to a dinner party during the fête planned by Boston in honor of Monteux's eightieth birthday. Ellen was humming the number one tune on the current Hit Parade.

"Oh, I know zat tune!" Monteux exclaimed in characteristic Parisian-English. *"Let Her Go!"*

Before he slept that night Fiedler pondered. If so serious a conductor as Monteux knew the Hit Parade tunes, he was right in assuming that they belonged in The Pops' repertory. He dipped into musical memory, hunting for songs with a common idea. His finished arrangement, running the gamut from Tosti's *Addio to Toot-toot-tootsie, Good-bye* sent a chuckling audience into the night whistling, and started a series of entertaining novelties. The most unique example of his laugh-exciting encores is probably *The Typewriter,* in which Joe Sinai finally threw the battered machine to the San Francisco Auditorium floor!

But Fiedler participation in the Monteux fête in 1955 was not in the Pops' vein. When the beloved Frenchman was asked to conduct a regular series concert on that auspicious birthday, Arthur called on him. "Mr. Monteux," he said, using the formality that has always remained since youthful homage to the Maestro. "What can I do for you?"

"Play for me again in ze viola section!" The octogenarian voice rang with old-time authority.

That brought uncomfortable memories and a hard stint of practicing. It seemed only yesterday, instead of over thirty years, since the flinty eyes of the Maestro had pierced his own when he came in late for a rehearsal.

And that had not been the only scolding "ze baddest boy in the orchestra" had had from the man who had later become his revered friend.

Arthur took his once-loved instrument from its silk wrappings in the case which had lain for years on the top shelf of his closet. He could not remember how long it had been since his busy schedule had allowed time for personal performance. He would make time now, and he put aside his scores and recordings, glad that he could shut two doors between his family and the necessary "wood-shedding." Those hours of struggle for perfection were long and difficult; but he was ready when Monteux pointed his baton to the viola section. The look the old master slanted his way said, "you are excused," as surely as the "zank you" when they met backstage after the concert!

That year found Arthur Fiedler participating for a second time in the winter series of the Boston Symphony Orchestra. On December 16, 1955—the day before his sixty-first birthday—he lifted his baton over the organization that had listed Fiedlers on its personnel file for seventy-one years. On that day he became the first Boston-born conductor, throughout its entire seventy-four-year history, to lead the Orchestra's regular Friday concert. Just once, twenty years before, on a Tuesday afternoon in 1935, the then versatile young "Poo Bah" had stepped to the podium when Koussevitzky was ill and Burgin had met with an automobile accident.

Since that emergency Fiedler fans had constantly

urged that he be given the courtesy of a guest invitation
for a regular series concert. The fiasco of the Villa Lobos
affair ten years later had fanned that flame; but except
for the request to lead the American Fund for Israel
concert, Koussevitzky had never seemed to regard his
colleague in any other light than that of an entertaining
Pops conductor. In the five years since Munch had taken
over the power exercized by Koussevitzky for a full quar-
ter-entury, he, too, had ignored the serious side of Arthur
Fiedler. This, despite the fact that by now the Pops conductor was, as many friends claimed, probably the best-
known American conductor in the world.

The very popularity that had come with world-
wide record sales, brilliant coast-to-coast Pops tours, and
the Fire Chief tradition, had hidden from public view
the earnest musician quietly collecting Haydn scores, and
biographies of great conductors. He was in a sense the
victim of his own success. Coursing through his veins
was ambition to be recognized as the rightful inheritor
of the name of the famous Nikisch and the meticulous
teacher, Emanuel Fiedler.

He had given his best where opportunity offered.
That best had brought tribute ranging from the child
who ran down the street to call his pals to see the picture
of "the man who makes the music" to the Governor of
Massachusetts; but an artist never truly succeeds until
he is acknowledged by his peers. When his services were
needed by a Sokoloff administering the National Music
Project, or a Stokowski organizing an American All-

Youth Orchestra, these men had turned to one who
never withheld his own energy if there were young artists
to encourage. But all this had been taken for granted too
long.

It was indeed "later than high time for this invitation," as Cyrus Durgin of the "Boston Globe" put it,
when at last Arthur Fiedler was Guest Conductor for the
home city orchestra. The program he chose for this day
portrayed the musician of his own dreams. Two members
were "firsts." One, Frescobaldi's *Toccata* (freely tran-
scribed by Hans Kindler) represented Fiedler research
into the past. The other, Kodaly's fresh and brilliant
Magyar gypsy tunes, gave release to the romanticist. His
guest pianist, Aldo Ciccolini, played Rachmaninoff's
Rhapsody on a Theme of Paganini, a favorite in which
Ruth Slenczynska had scored triumphs across the United
States with his tours. The glorious Beethoven *Eighth*
highlighted the afternoon.

Durgin summed up the complete effect in words
that showed discernment of what Fiedler had to offer
the receptive listener: "Between the live, compact,
blended and 'unfussed' tones of the orchestra and the
sight of Mr. Fiedler's spare, dominating and expert baton
technique, it was plain that we were enjoying the work
of a most able conductor. . . . All was healthy, vigorous,
but not coarse."

Fiedler's Silver Jubilee Year brought recognition
in varied forms. The fifty-thousand visitors to the Boston
Arts Festival in the Public Gardens had seen his name

linked with poet Robert Frost among the honorees. They had crowded the free concert conducted by the Pops Maestro as the concluding highlight of the Festival. San Francisco had held special ceremonies to make Arthur Fiedler an honorary citizen. France had elected him a *Chevalier of the Legion of Honor*.

Five years later he received a second honorary PhD—from a small but historically important college in Springfield, Massachusetts, the city that had first offered young Arthur Fiedler a chance to earn money in America. The now successful Pops conductor accepted this honor humbly as he thought of the service of The American International College, established in the mid-eighties to educate French-Canadians in the United States, and now enrolling students from places as far apart as Jordan and the Philippines. Recognition from a college which had an overseas branch in the Azores seemed fitting to a man whose musical mission had become international.

That same winter the Otoe Indians of Stillwater, Oklahoma, made him Honorary Chief of their tribe, with the name, *Maker of Sweet Music*; while at the June Commencement of Ripon College in Wisconsin, he walked in the academic procession beside equally handsome actor Frederic March to receive the degree of *Doctor of Fine Arts*. He wears these hoods with unassuming gratitude, but is "Dr." Fiedler only if an engagement takes him to a University campus.

Tributes to the organization he serves are of greater importance. He stood beside Charles Munch in the Senate of the Commonwealth of Massachusetts on the seventy-fifth birthday of the Boston Symphony Orchestra to hear citations which said: "Both orchestras under their leaders have enriched the lives of people through the world and have brought greater respect and appreciation for the cultural reputation of the people of Massachusetts." Then the two men jointly accepted the diamond-studded baton from L. W. Kanaga, Vice President of RCA-Victor, in commemoration of the forty-years association of the Symphony with that organization.

Unnoticed in these busy years had been the passing of Arthur Fiedler's sixty-fifth birthday. Retirement is an unused word in the Pops Maestro's vocabulary, in spite of the fact that nature has made some protests. Major surgery in 1955 and two severe thrombosis attacks in recent years have been accepted and conquered by this man of seemingly inexhaustible energy. When the physician told Ellen after the first heart attack, "Your husband will open The Pops Season, or you will have a chronic invalid on your hands," he understood the deepest need of Arthur Fiedler. Constructive work in the realm of music is essential to his life; and so he built himself back, step by step, to fulfill his purpose. Evening after evening the two Fiedlers walked together along tree-shaded Brookline streets, adding a block at a time until his strength returned.

He has an iron will that triumphs over any physical ailment. When a flu attack sent him to bed with a fever of 104 degrees on a cold San Francisco July night, he woke at the sound of a 4:00 a.m. phone call in Ellen's adjoining room. "What was that?" he demanded, taking the phone from her in time to hear the word, FIRE! (Operators in ninety cities now have orders to call the Honorary Fire Chief for any four-alarm conflagration.) He was dressed and off in the fog, paying no attention to her protest. The next morning he was at rehearsal, as full of pep as ever!

Tireless effort remains his watchword, whether the demand be from vocation or avocation; and symbols of appreciation from recipients continue to fill home and office shelves. A large silver bowl inscribed:

To Arthur Fiedler
with the
Gratitude and Affection
of the
Revere High School Choral Club

took its place next to the silver plate given him fifteen years earlier when he retired as Director of The Cecilia. That plate bears the same marking as his bachelor silver —a bar of music, with "a"-"f" in notes; but the recent bowl continues to say: "In appreciation for enriching our Lives by his Brilliant and Dedicated Leadership of the Boston Pops Orchestra. For his Interest in Youth and for Encouraging the Participation of the Revere High School Choral Club on his Program."

On the front hall table a large illuminated placque

from *Junior Achievement* of Boston likewise recognizes
his inspiration to youth. The lamp which lights the
library desk bears signatures of his Pops players on its
parchment shade; and an autographed photograph of
Toscanini hangs next to the gold *Jalousie* record. But
among all the accumulated mementoes perhaps the engrossed copy of a resolution passed by the Congress of
the United States best summarizes the gratitude of all
Americans. This was introduced in the spring of 1959
by Senators John F. Kennedy and Leverett Saltonstall,
and Congressman Laurence Curtis to congratulate Arthur
Fiedler on his thirtieth anniversary as Conductor of The
Pops—a tenure which they characterized as "to our
knowledge the longest current association of conductor
and orchestra anywhere in the world."

RESOLUTION HONORING ARTHUR FIEDLER ON
HIS THIRTIETH ANNIVERSARY AS CONDUCTOR
OF THE BOSTON POPS CONCERTS

Whereas: Arthur Fiedler, a native born American, has been
     conductor of the Boston Pops Concerts for 30 years, one
     of the longest tenures in musical history, and
Whereas: Arthur Fiedler's personality, flair and sound musi-
     cianship have made these concerts known throughout
     the world, and
Whereas: Arthur Fiedler has made an enormous world public
     aware of the charm and satisfactions of good popular
     music played by a symphony orchestra, and
Whereas: In these 30 years Arthur Fiedler has led over 2,000

concerts in this country and abroad heard by audiences of many millions, and

Whereas: Arthur Fiedler has spread the pleasure of music to millions more by means of radio, television, and sound recordings, and

Whereas: Arthur Fiedler and the Boston Pops Orchestra in these 30 years have come to occupy a unique position in the musical history of Boston, the United States of America, and the world.

Therefore: be it resolved: That the Senate (The House of Representatives concurring) of the United States of America hereby heartily congratulates Arthur Fiedler on his thirtieth anniversary as conductor of the Boston Pops Concerts and expresses the gratitude of the nation for his contribution to our cultural life and musical heritage.

When The Pops opened that April, Frank Hatch spoke for the Board of Trustees of the Boston Symphony as he presented a beautifully bound first edition of *Don Giovanni,* insribed to Arthur Fiedler as their gift. His message to the conductor was phrased in his own verse, concluding:

> "Encore, encore
> For thirty more
> Before we say adieu.
> Drive carefully
> And live to be
> Another Pierre Monteux."

In its report of the occasion, the "Boston Daily Record" observed: "Forthwith Fiedler made one of his quick bows, then turned his wordless back to the orchestra; for as the late Nicholas Young of these papers once said of him, 'Arthur Fiedler is not afflicted with public speaking.' "

But he comes near to being "a source of perpetual motion," as Cyrus Durgin described him on his return from the 1962 Boston Pops Tour Orchestra trek of eleven-thousand miles through twenty states. His only concession to reasonable thought of his own well being came that summer. Instead of making an extra transcontinental jet round trip to give his services as conductor of a benefit concert for the Children's Health Council of Palo Alto, as he had done in two previous summers, he insisted that it be scheduled immediately after the close of the San Francisco Pops season.

Daylight saving meant that at five o'clock the August sun still poured warmth onto the grassy slopes of Stanford University's beautiful Lawrence Frost Memorial Amphitheatre as ten thousand Bay Area music lovers wound their way up tree-lined paths to hear Summer Symphony No. 3. The writer of the program notes had used Walt Whitman's words perceptively. "When I give, I give of myself" is exactly what that figure in the gray sports coat was doing as Fiedler, oblivious to the heat, picked up his baton to lead Wagner's *Entrance of the Guests into the Wartburg* from *Tannhauser*. Copland and Strauss, Offenbach and Bernstein, Tchaikovsky (played by guest pianist, Roy Bogas, with the orchestra) were blended into a program that ended with this latest

medley of TV Westerns—*Pops Round-up*. Evening
shadows dappled Stanford Hills and the mellifluous
sound of the Belgian carillon in the Hoover Tower
floated across the Amphitheatre as a grateful audience
pressed forward to thank this man who would give so
much to help handicapped children.

Because he is so modest, few of these people could
know that he has been giving with the same gallantry all
of his life. From adolescent appearances in Berlin benefits to the fruitful Grenfell Mission Nights at the openings of The Pops, Fiedler generosity has made life more
meaningful for all manner of people. Gratitude is not
always spelled out as it was in the Palo Alto Program. It
comes in the press of a handshake or with an extra pound
of mushrooms when he shops in Boston's North End.
And sometimes his response to a request brings unexpected results. He is all too willing to do a favor if the
asker is a friend. That is how he hit the wire services
with the Twist picture.

A trumpeter in the San Francisco Pops orchestra
said casually, "A few of us play at Club '365.' Maybe on
one of your night prowls, you'd like to drop in." Arthur
and Joe Sinai did just that one night.

"Do you dance The Twist?" someone asked.
"Sure," and he stepped out with the singer.

A girl pointed a camera. "Mind if I take your
picture?" "Go ahead," he smiled affably, thinking it was
just a personal candid shot.

The next morning he picked up the paper from his breakfast tray. "What!" he almost spilled the coffee. "There I am!"

And in Brookline the postman began delivering clippings to Ellen from newspapers all over the country.

"Who is the dame?" she teased when her husband arrived home. "Can't even remember her name," he replied honestly. "I only spoke to her about two minutes."

Despite the image created by photographers and publicity men, Arthur Fiedler is neither a buffoon nor a comedian. He is a sincere, selective and sensitive musician—a mature evolution of the rigidly diciplined son of Emanuel Fiedler. And yet he has no adequate realization of the magnitude of his accomplishments. It is difficult to draw from him any incident that reveals recognition of his musical excellence. The story of Stravinsky's autographed thanks for "the best performance of this that I have ever heard" on a score of *The Symphony of Psalms* slipped inadvertently into conversation. He apologized for mentioning it.

Bronze or stone would provide static monuments to this dynamic human being. He would seem unreal on a pedestal such as that which commemorates Mozart in the Salzburg Platz, or wreathed in bronze as is Strauss with his violin in Vienna. Unlike these compatriots of his forefathers, Arthur Fiedler has been honored by his native city with a characteristically utilitarian tribute.

At the base of a concrete ramp winding over Stor-

row Drive where the freeway curves along The Esplanade
is a simple bronze plaque. On it a bas relief of his face
looks at the words:

ARTHUR FIEDLER BRIDGE

Erected in 1953, the 25th year of The Esplanade Concerts.
Named in honor of their creator and conductor.
Devoting his musical gift to the service of the public in his
native community, he has here brought music of the masters
to countless thousands in these concerts, the first to be played
each summer by a major symphony orchestra, free to all.

In the lower left hand corner is a bar of music
from *The Love Death of Tristan and Isolde,* commenc-
ing with "a"-"f." The plaque is signed by Christian
Herter, Governor of the Commonwealth of Massachusetts. This is indeed a fitting sequel to the faith of
that other Governor, Alvan Fuller, who backed his
imaginative young friend a quarter of a century earlier.
Summer after summer for more than a decade this
bridge has brought thousands safely above speeding cars
to spend two carefree hours under the spell of the great
music of the ages. A tiny black-faced girl in stiffly-
starched pink gingham clings to the hand of her wrinkled
grandmother. The soft orange silk sari of an East Indian
student blows in the river breeze. A young mother in
Capris pushes a stroller up the ramp. An old man leans
heavily on his cane while two 'teen-agers in shorts jostle
by. The sky is softly mauve above the white columns of

M.I.T., and brown smoke drifts from the stacks of a plant nearby.

When the music is over, the crowd starts back in reverse. Sleeping babies cling to their fathers' necks and young people mount the ramp hand-in-hand. Stranger speaks to stranger. "Did you enjoy the concert?" and some one pushes by whistling an air from *Finlandia*.

Arthur Fiedler is busily autographing programs for admirers who have lingered back of the Shell. He cannot hear the rumble of feet going over the bridge; but if he could, he might discern the theme of a song they would all like to sing:

"Thank you, 'Mr. Pops.' You have become Music's great apostle!"

Current RCA Victor Records

by Arthur Fiedler

LM/LSC-2130   J. Strauss, Jr.: Die Fledermaus and Gypsy Baron
              Excerpts
LM/LSC-2202   Pops Caviar
LM/LSC-2229   Marches in Hi-Fi
LM/LSC-2267   Offenbach: Gaite Parisienne; Khachaturian:
              Gayne Ballet Suite
LM/LSC-2329   Pops Christmas Party
LM/LSC-2367   Gershwin: Rhapsody in Blue; An American in
              Paris
LM/LSC-2380   Music from Million Dollar Movies
LM/LSC-2439   Fiedler's All-Time Favorites
LM/LSC-2442   The Music of Franz Liszt
LM/LSC-2546   Liebestraum
LM/LSC-2547   Light Classics
LM/LSC-2548   Viennese Night
LM/LSC-2549   Family Fun with Familiar Music
LM/LSC-2556   Hearts in ¾ Time
LM/LSC-2586   Gershwin: Concerto in F; Cuban Overture; "I
              Got Rhythm" Variations
LM/LSC-2595   Pops Roundup
LM/LSC-2596   Saint-Saens: Carnival of the Animals; Britten:
              The Young Person's Guide to the Orchestra
LM/LSC-2604   Opera Without Singing
LM/LSC-2621   Prokofieff: Love for Three Oranges; Chopin:
              Les Sylphides
LM/LSC-2638   Leroy Anderson Favorites
LM/LSC-2661   "Jalousie" and Other Favorites in the Latin
              Flavor
LM/LSC-2670   Star Dust
LM/LSC-2677   Concert in the Park
LM/LSC-2678   Litolff: Concerto Symphonique No. 4: Scherzo;
              Franck: Symphonic Variations; Rachmani-
              noff: Paganini Rhapsody, Op. 43

LM/LSC-2688	Tchaikovsky: Swan Lake
LM/LSC-2729	"Pops" Goes the Trumpet (with Al Hirt as soloist)
LM/LSC-2744	Favorite Dances and Marches
LM/LSC-2745	Music America Loves Best
LM/LSC-2746	Rhapsody
LM/LSC-2747	Slaughter on Tenth Avenue and Other Hits from the Big Shows
LM/LSC-2757	The World's Greatest Marches (album in collaboration with the Boston Symphony Orchestra, Erich Leinsdorf conducting)
LM/LSC-2773	Peter and the Commissar (with Allan Sherman as soloist)
LM/LSC-2782	More Music from Million Dollar Movies
LM/LSC-2789	Grofe: Grand Canyon Suite; Bernstein: Candide Overture; 2 Pops Favorites
LM/LSC-2798	Tenderly
LM/LSC-2810	The Best of Arthur Fiedler and the Boston Pops
LM/LSC-2817	Gold: Music from "Ship of Fools"
LM/LSC-2821	Nero Goes "Pops" (with Peter Nero, pianist)
LM/LSC-2827	An Evening at the "Pops"
LM/LSC-2857	Ellington: The Duke at Tanglewood (Duke Ellington, pianist)
LM/LSC-2870	The "Pops" Goes Country (Chet Atkins, guitarist)
LM/LSC-2882	More Highlights from an Evening at the "Pops"
LM/LSC-2885	Holiday for Strings
LM/LSC-2906	All the Things You Are
LM/LSC-2925	Stan Getz and Arthur Fiedler at Tanglewood
LM/LSC-2928	Tales from Vienna
LM/LSC-2946	Irish Night at the "Pops"
LM/LSC-2965	Music from Million Dollar Movies